RENÉE OF FRANCE

RENÉE
OF FRANCE

Simonetta Carr

PUBLISHING WITH A MISSION

EP BOOKS
Faverdale North
Darlington
DL3 0PH, England

www.epbooks.org
sales@epbooks.org

EP BOOKS are distributed in the USA by:
JPL Distribution
3741 Linden Avenue Southeast
Grand Rapids, MI 49548.

E-mail: orders@jpldistribution.com
Tel: 877.683.6935

First published 2013

British Library Cataloguing in Publication Data available
ISBN: 978-0-85234-909-0

Contents

TIMELINE

25 October 1510   Renée is born.

1514   Renée's mother, Anne of Brittany, dies. Her only sister Claude marries Francis of Angoulême.

1515   Renée's father, King Louis XII of France, dies. Francis of Angoulême inherits the crown as King Francis I.

31 October 1517   Martin Luther nails his *95 Theses* to the church door in Wittenberg.

1527   The sack of Rome by some forces of Emperor Charles V shakes Europe.

1528   Renée marries Duke Ercole II of Este and moves to Ferrara, Italy.

1529	Charles V signs the Treaty of Barcelona with the pope and the Treaty of Cambrai with France, leaving Ferrara out of the picture.
1531	Birth of Renée's first child, Anna.
1533	Birth of Renée's second child, Alfonso, heir to the duchy of Este.
1534	Protestant extremists plaster Paris with posters against the Roman Catholic Mass, causing a strong reaction. The ensuing persecution brings many refugees to Renée.
1534	Duke Alfonso I of Este dies and Ercole II inherits the duchy.
1535	Birth of Renée's third child, Lucrezia.
1536	John Calvin visits Ferrara.
1537	Birth of Renée's fourth child, Leonora.
1539	Birth of Renée's fifth child and second son, Luigi.
1540	Ercole gives Renée a villa in Consandolo.
1542	The Roman inquisition is re-established.

1543	Pope Paul III arrives in Ferrara and signs an agreement with Renée, allowing her to be tried directly by the ecclesiastical authorities in Rome.
1548	Anna marries Francis, Duke of Guise, in Paris.
1549	Protestant Fanino Fanini is arrested in Ferrara. Renée repeatedly pleads with her husband for mercy.
1550	Julius III becomes pope. Fanini is hung and burned. Luigi d'Este becomes Bishop of Ferrara.
1551	The Lord's Supper begins to be celebrated in Renée's villa in Consandolo.
1559	Ercole dies.
7 November 1560	Renée arrives in Orléans, France.
December 1560	King Francis II of France dies. His brother Charles IX succeeds him (under the care of his mother, Catherine de' Medici).
January 1561	Renée moves to Montargis.
September–October 1561	The Colloquy of Poissy fails to reconcile Huguenots (French Protestants) and Catholics.

January 1562	The Edict of Saint-Germain pronounces some tolerance toward the Huguenots.
March 1562	The Duke of Guise attacks a Protestant church in Vassy. The first of the French Wars of Religion starts.
February 1563	The Duke of Guise asks Renée to leave Montargis. She tries to buy time and, on 24 February, the duke dies from a wound.
1563	The Treaty of Amboise ends the First War of Religion.
27 April 1564	John Calvin dies.
1567-1568	Second War of Religion.
1568	The Edict of St Maur prohibits all religions but Catholicism.
1568-1570	Third War of Religion.
1572	Tensions mount in Paris over the wedding between Henri of Navarre and Marguerite of Valois. They culminate in the St Bartholomew's Day Massacre of Huguenots. Renée barely escapes, returning to Montargis.
1572-1573	Fourth War of Religion.

1574   Charles IX dies; Henri III becomes king
                  of France.

12 June 1575   Renée dies.

INTRODUCTION

A bruised reed he will not break,
and a faintly burning wick he will not quench
(Isaiah 42:3).

The influence of the Protestant Reformation still permeates much of our Western culture. At the same time, our popular perception of that complex, fluid, and transformative time is often rigid and simplistic. Perhaps it might be easier to grasp if we try to experience it through the struggles, desires, perplexities, convictions, and quests of someone who lived though it — in this case, a vocal and inquisitive woman — Renée of France. Although Renée belonged to the nobility of that time, the course of events kept her focused on some basic questions of faith — the same ones that many of us face. Is faith a private matter? Can we just believe secretly in our hearts? What harm is there in a little pretence? In fact, should we not hide and suppress some aspects of our faith if they offend others?

What did Christ mean when he told us to love our enemies? What is the role of the church in our life, especially when we are placed in a position of responsibility? How can God forgive us when we utterly deny him? And how can we ever get back on our feet?

A major element in Renée's life is her correspondence with the French Reformer, John Calvin, which continues for most of her life and opens a window on less familiar aspects of his soul. Of all his correspondence with women, his letters to Renée are unique, revealing a close bond of friendship. Calvin often feels free to reveal his struggles to her in a way he would not do with others, and she talks openly and trustingly about her puzzlement, fear, and exasperation. In the background, the distinctive struggles of the Reformation in Italy and France evolve rapidly before our eyes.

Who was Renée of France? For some, she was a devoted daughter of the Church of Rome, misled and deceived by John Calvin and other reformers. For others, a heroine of the Reformation, who kept her faith — with the exception of one painful lapse — in spite of fierce persecution. Some, emphasizing her complaints to Calvin in her last letters, have described her as a free or ecumenical spirit. For many, she is difficult to categorize. Unlike most religious heroes of her time, she seems uncertain, wavering, insecure, ambiguous and divided in her loyalties.

She was not a powerful leader like Marguerite of Navarre or Jeanne d'Albret. Unlike many other noblewomen of her time, she did not leave any writings except for a few letters, often disorganized in thought. Her physical appearance was considered disappointing. She has been described as homely, with a noticeably unpleasant deformation of the spine.

Her behaviour was puzzling even to some of her contemporaries. Right when Jesuits were exultantly taking the credit for her return to the Roman Catholic faith, Protestants were writing her praises as a faithful patroness. By the time she returned to France, where Calvinism was becoming institutionalized and noblewomen were taking the lead in its promotion, Huguenots described Renée as hesitant and uncommitted. On the other hand, her son Alfonso could not give her a proper Catholic funeral because she died as an unrepentant Protestant.

Some see her importance only on a strategic level. As a French princess and Italian duchess, she was sought by both Protestant and Catholic leaders (chiefly John Calvin and Ignatius of Loyola) as a possible tool to influence the nobility in both countries.

The poet Clement Marot saw her as a sad and lonely woman in need of help and understanding. Child prodigy and scholar Olympia Morata saw her as an irresolute ruler who failed to protect her from slanders and whose fall did not come as a surprise. The Jesuit Jean Pelletier described her as theologically ignorant and unprepared, while many introductions to Italian Protestant works hail her as a wise and knowledgeable discerner of Scriptures.

Through her correspondence we get some glimpses of her soul — sharing the simple joy of wrestling with an impertinent puppy in her younger days, the deep confusion of her middle years, and her vexation toward her critics and outrage at the horrors of war toward the end of her life. The glimpses are sometimes indirect, because most of her letters have been destroyed and — as someone has remarked — trying to interpret a voice through a correspondent's answers is like listening to a person talking to someone else on the phone and trying to guess what the other party is saying.

It is also easy to perceive some unspoken feelings through the events of her life. Parents, and especially mothers, can readily sense, or at least imagine, her pain as she faced the piercing opposition of her oldest son, as well as her feelings of powerlessness as she watched her oldest daughter marry a fierce promoter of Roman Catholicism and her youngest son embrace a clerical career in the Church of Rome. In the end, after all her efforts, none of her children openly shared her faith.

Who, then, was Renée of France? This book does not attempt to give a definitive answer. It just offers a brief look at the life of a woman who made difficult choices and asked stimulating questions — someone like most of us, often baffled by uncertainties, resisting changes, stubborn, and frustrated. Some of us may recognize themselves in her struggles as a wife, mother, or ruler. Some may find comfort in the pastoral advice she received and especially share her deep gratefulness to God who, 'purely by his goodness and liberality', has preserved her and us until now.

The first nine chapters in this book describe the major events of her life, giving a quick background of Renée's childhood and youth and focusing on the years between her wedding to Duke Ercole and her death. Throughout them, we notice the constancy of Calvin's pastoral encouragement, which is developed more specifically in chapter ten. There, I have compiled some of Calvin's counsel into topics, some particularly urgent at that time but still relevant today (the Mass, religious simulation, and church government and discipline), and some more specifically related to Renée's questions (love for our enemies, the unity of the Old and New Testaments, and relying on God's strength in the discharging of our duties).

In conformity to the other titles in this series, this book contains very few footnotes and references to other works. It is not an academic study, and is based mostly on the correspondence between Renée and John Calvin and on secondary sources. The English translation of this correspondence and other Italian or French sources has been done by the author.

I have many people to thank for their part in the making of this book — Dr Michael Haykin and the editors at Evangelical Press for initially suggesting this title; Prof. Dr Herman J. Selderhuis, professor of church history and church polity at the Theological University, Apeldoorn, and Dr Emanuele Fiume, researcher and author on church history (particularly on Italian Protestantism), for checking the original manuscript and writing careful endorsements; my friend Heather Chisholm-Chait for her careful editing and thought-provoking questions; my friend Dianna Ippolito for her promptings and suggestions; Nazareno Ulfo, Director at Alfa e Omega publishers, for providing me with a copy of their book *Lealtà in Tensione* (see bibliography for details); my friends Emanuele Taglietti and Katia Petronelli, for providing me with a copy of the journal *Schifanoia*; my friends Dr George F. Carnevale, research scientist at UCSD and John O' Connor, a graduate of UCSD, for their help in obtaining valuable articles and a doctoral dissertation available only through university libraries' inter-loans. I am also deeply grateful to Emanuele Taglietti for producing, in record time and as a rare gesture of enduring friendship, an enchanting painting for the cover of this book.

1

A STORMY MARRIAGE

Born again in name and in soul — child of king by birth,
child of heaven by knowledge of Him who will save her
(Clement Marot, 1496–1544, poet).[1]

The sudden thunder of hooves shook the quietness of the late-summer night. Soon the villa in Consandolo, Italy, became a hive of activity as everyone assembled in the hall to hear Duke Ercole's decree. The orders were peremptory. His wife Renée was to return immediately to the palace in Ferrara, taking only two of her servants. Their daughters Lucrezia and Eleonora would be transported to the monastery of Corpus Christi in nearby Modena. Everyone else had two hours to leave the villa or they would be arrested and tried. All books, documents, and letters would be taken to the Inquisitor for inspection.

We can only imagine some of the thoughts that crowded Renée's mind as she climbed into the carriage. The guards, on the other hand, reported that she was *allegrissima* (very cheerful).

Choosing to believe one single record written at a time when historical accuracy was not a priority is treading on unstable ground. However, Renée might have smiled. Maybe she felt confident. She had generally been able to do as she pleased and had filled her palace with Protestant refugees in spite of the duke's opposition. Maybe she thought that this, too, would easily pass.

She might also have felt relieved, seeing long-standing tensions come to a head. Or maybe her smile was simply a smile of defiance, depriving the duke of the satisfaction of seeing her crushed by his hostility.

From princess to duchess

Most probably, Renée remembered vividly her first meeting with Duke Ercole II of Este (1508–1559) in Paris twenty-six years earlier, just a month before their wedding. She was not yet eighteen at the time, and he was barely twenty. The encounter had been awkward for both. Orphaned from childhood — her father, King Louis XII of France (1462–1515), and her mother, Anne, Duchess of Brittany (1477–1514), had both died before she was five — Renée had also lost her only sibling: her older sister Claude (1499–1524). Technically, had she been born a man or had France not passed the Salic law forbidding women to inherit the throne, she should have been on the throne of France instead of marrying the heir-apparent of a small Italian duchy, and she knew it all too well.

Arranged marriages were, however, one of the burdens of nobility, and Renée had been prepared for this day from birth. Other noblemen had been considered as spouses, such as England's King Henry VIII (1491–1547) and Charles of Austria (1500–1558), who at the time of her wedding had become Emperor Charles V of the Holy Roman Empire, but none of these possibilities had materialized.

Though small, Ferrara was a prestigious state; and King Francis I (1494–1547), Claude's husband and heir to Louis XII's throne, understood its strategic value as a political ally. Conscious of the sacrifice he was asking of Renée, he undoubtedly reassured her that he would always be there to help her, sending money and servants as she needed them and mediating difficult situations.

Ercole's father, on the other hand, Duke Alfonso I of Este (1476–1534), was convinced that an alliance with France would guarantee peace and independence to his duchy, especially from the Emperor and the Pope, to whom the Este family still owed fealty. Particularly, the invasion of Italy and conquest of Rome[2] by Charles V's armies the previous year had left Italian rulers trembling for their safety.

Ercole was not sure. Trained to understand politics from a young age, he had learned that treaties are too easily broken. Besides, he was not impressed with Renée's looks. A handsome young man, with a passion for hunting, theatre, and adventure, he had been surrounded by beautiful art, landscapes, architecture, and women from birth, starting with the renowned looks of his mother, Lucrezia Borgia (1480–1519). After meeting his bride, he wrote to his father very frankly, 'Madame Renée is not beautiful, but she might make up for this with other good qualities.'

After a magnificent wedding on 28 June 1528 at Aix-la-Chapelle, near Paris, the newly-weds remained at the royal court for the rest of the summer. A pestilence had just hit Ferrara, and it was not safe to return. Renée probably enjoyed the opportunity to spend a few more months at home, savouring for the last time familiar places and friends. On the other hand, King Francis had begun to receive upsetting news about the dissatisfaction of some of his hired captains in Italy, one of whom[3] had just defected, entering the service of Charles V. Recognizing the urgency of those matters, he tried hard to get the newly-wed couple out of France as soon as possible.

As the first hints of autumn coloured the land, Renée took her old governess, Michelle de Saubonne, and a large entourage of about 150 courtiers, and left with Ercole on their long journey to Italy. Saubonne, better known as Madame de Soubise, had been like a mother to the young Renée after working for several years as maid-of-honour to her mother Anne. Dismissed from court, on account of some disagreements, by Louise of Savoy (1476–1531), King Francis' mother, she had been called back by Renée on the occasion of her wedding, and kept at her service as closest confidante. Some believe she was the first prominent French noblewoman to have openly professed her Calvinist faith.

The young couple and their large entourage (Ercole had come to Paris with a train of at least two hundred people) proceeded slowly through the southern part of France, crossing the Alps just before the weather became too inclement. Then they continued through the north of Italy, stopping on their way at the invitations of other noblemen. It was already November when they approached Ferrara, a time when a thick fog normally takes residence in the Po valley, transforming familiar objects into eerie sights. Duke Alfonso met them several miles away and escorted them, after another short stop, to his court.

In Ferrara, the citizens had been preparing for the princess's arrival. Duke Alfonso had instructed everyone to dress in cheerful fashion so as to mask the dreadful effects of the plague. The royal barge, however, arrived much later than expected, so the celebrations were postponed to the following day.

The castle of Ferrara, a formidable medieval stronghold with four red, imposing towers, surrounded by a greenish moat, was very different from the magnificent and newly renovated castle of Blois where Renée was born and the royal residences at Amboise and Fontainebleau where she had spent some of her life. It had originally been built as a fortress to protect the duchy from its enemies, and not as a monument to pomp and splendour.

Soon she became acquainted with its spacious halls, its rooms, and its gardens. She especially loved the orange garden on the first floor, a terrace with orange trees in large vases, which were moved inside every winter. She probably walked to the top of the towers to survey the city, and became at least aware of the location of the prisons. In one prison, Alfonso's brothers Giulio (1478–1561) and Ferrante (1477–1540) were kept on a charge of treason, never visited by any of the Este family.

In the courtyard, she surveyed the cannons ready to defend the fortress from any attack and the infamous place where Parisina, the teenage wife of aged Marquis Niccolò III (1383–1441), had been beheaded with her lover, Niccolò's young son. Over time, Renée visited all the Este residences (or 'delizie') in the area, used as summer residences, for hunting trips, or simply as get-aways. Every Sunday, she attended Mass at the castle's chapel or at the sumptuous nearby cathedral.

She most probably visited the University of Ferrara, one of the oldest in Europe, where fertile minds such as those of Nicolaus Copernicus (1473–1543) and Paracelsus (1493–1541) had contributed to shaping the cultural and scientific thought of Renaissance Europe.

Those dangerous French

Renée might have learned some Italian before arriving in Ferrara because, as cradle of the Renaissance, Italy was sought after as a place of art and learning, and Italian was commonly studied around Europe. We know that she had a good knowledge of Latin and Greek, and had received a thorough education in liberal arts and several sciences.

At any rate, even if Renée eventually learned to speak and read Italian well, French remained her language of choice.

She built, in fact, a distinctively French court around her, where everyone spoke French and dressed according to the French fashion, in her eyes much more modest than the Italian. Most of all, she found comfort in the company of her governess and in her correspondence with old friends back in France, particularly Marguerite of Navarre (1492–1549), King Francis' sister, who had always been her close companion and adviser. Marguerite, a patron of the arts and of religious reformation, had introduced to the royal court several French pre-reformers such as Jacques Lefèvre D'Étaples (*c*. 1455–1536) and Guillaume Briçonnet (*c*. 1472–1534), firm believers in justification by faith alone.

Duke Alfonso, an affable and generous man, was generally accommodating toward his new daughter-in-law, while Ercole quickly became impatient with the French flavour of her court. They both agreed, however, on the seriousness of the financial drain she was exercising on their treasury, as she insisted in paying her subjects according to French standards, lavishing expensive clothes on them. It did not help the situation that in July 1529, Charles V signed the Treaty of Barcelona with the pope and, in August, the Treaty of Cambrai with Francis I, each time leaving Ferrara to fend for itself, in spite of the marriage between Ercole and Renée.

Renée reacted to Ercole's irritation by surrounding herself with more French courtiers, servants, and teachers. Some were Protestants who had to escape France, especially after the fateful night between October 17 and 18, 1534, when some religious extremists plastered Paris and other towns with posters violently condemning the Roman Catholic

Mass, and even moderate Lutherans became a target of retaliation by French authorities.

The event, known as the *Affaire des placards*, provoked a harsh response even from King Francis, who had until then been tolerant of new religious views but reacted with fury when he found one poster plastered to his bedchamber door in Amboise. At this point, Marguerite's intervention, always effective in the past, was of no avail. A list of dangerous Lutherans was posted. Some were killed in a public execution, King Francis presiding, and others managed to flee. A notable refugee who fled to Ferrara at this time was Clement Marot (1496–1544), a renowned humanist and poet who had until then enjoyed the protection of the king in spite of his religious views.

For the most part, Ercole did not concern himself with the religious persuasion of his courtiers, as long as they were useful to enhance the prestige and cultural level of his duchy. He had, however, some personal friction with the Soubise 'clan', who had acquired powerful positions as attendants to his wife. He apparently resented their attitude (Madame de Soubise in particular seemed to have a dominating personality) and the high salaries they received (for Madame, 1200 *livres tournois* per year, as opposed to 200 given to secretary and poet Léon Jamet). Most of all, he feared that they were acting as spies for King Francis.

That is why, when Duke Alfonso died on 31 October 1534, Renée began to seriously expect an attack by Ercole on her household. Her suspicions soon proved right. The signs were subtle at first. Some letters to France were being intercepted.

Later, Ercole started to impose taxes on objects imported from France for her household.

Everything came to a head in the autumn of 1535, when Ercole visited Rome and Naples to orchestrate some agreements with both the new pope, Paul III (1468–1549), and the emperor. While there, he discovered that his brother Ippolito (1479–1520) had plans to leave for France on a trip closely related to Ercole's present discussions. Renée's encouragement of these plans was the last straw. When the duke returned to Ferrara in January 1536, he was shocked to find that Renée was preparing to meet the French court in Lyons, as they travelled to Milan to assess their claims on that city. To him, it was all a political plot against him.

His fears may have had some reasonable grounds. France might have seen his new alliance with both the pope and the emperor with displeasure, and a letter by Marguerite advising Renée to travel lightly during her trip might have suggested that the duchess was thinking of taking flight. It would not have been unusual. The mistreatment of wives on religious accounts was not uncommon at that time (Renée's case was actually less tragic than others), and Martin Luther (1483–1546), history's most famous reformer, had conceded that unbearable circumstances could be a warrant for separation.[4]

Immediately, Ercole expelled the Soubises from his court, except for Michelle's daughter Anne de Parthenay (d. 1556), because her husband Antoine de Pons (1510–1586) had an important position in his service. He also flatly forbade Renée from travelling. From then on, he continued to look at each French member of Renée's court with suspicion.

One of the French courtiers who were sent away around that time was Clement Marot, who moved briefly to Venice, where he wrote a letter to King Francis asking him to allow him back in his country. The persecution had relaxed by then, so the king gave his permission. From Venice, Marot also wrote to Marguerite a poem about Renée, which gives us an idea of her feelings at that time.

> Ah, Marguerite, listen to the sufferings
> Of the noble heart of Renée of France,
> Then, as a sister stronger than hope,
> Console her![5]

The duke's criteria in expelling the French Protestants from court are evident in his treatment of Léon Jamet, one of Marot's dearest friends. Jamet had also come to Italy at the time of the French persecution but, because of the invaluable help lent to the duke during his negotiations with the pope, he was kept in Rome as one of Ercole's agents and then promptly readmitted at the Este court. While his name appeared on the list of heretics in the rough draft of one of Ercole's letters, it was later erased and is not seen in the final version.

2

A FATEFUL VISIT

Therefore Madame, to whom God has given in his infinite mercy the knowledge of his name, enlightening you in the truth of his holy Gospel, you are to fulfil your vocation (John Calvin).

Most sources give 1536 as the year when John Calvin (1509–1564) visited Ferrara. We do not know which month, nor for how long, but we can imagine that, given the difficulties of those times, his stay was quite brief. We know, however, that he played safe by using a different name, Charles d'Esperville.

An unsettling guest

Calvin and Renée had much in common. They were almost the same age (Calvin was one year older), both French, and both away from their land. We do not have any record of the discussions between them at this time, nor of the nature of his visit. It is possible that he was sent to Renée, like many other religious refugees at that time, by Marguerite of Navarre. It is also possible that he was hoping to find in Renée another influential voice able to persuade King Francis to put to an end the persecution of Protestants in France. Given that his recent *Institutes of the Christian Religion* had been dedicated to Francis, we know that Calvin had hopes that the monarch could understand and perhaps even support the Reformers' cause, just as in the past he had often intervened to mitigate the attacks against Protestants by conservative faculty members at the Sorbonne.

Calvin's visit had a profound impact on Renée and her court. This was evident in the prolonged correspondence between him and the duchess, who continued to hold the Reformer and his advice in high regard until her death. It was, throughout Europe, a time of questions and debates, with new ideas and interpretations springing up at every corner, and Calvin's clarity and lucid logic might have given Renée some comforting stability.

Calvin probably discussed and summarized his *Institutes* for the small community of believers in Renée's court. We know from later letters that one of the subjects of these discussions was the practice of the Roman Catholic Mass, which he saw as an abomination and idolatry in God's eyes. It is possible, then, to trace to his teachings the open defiance of some members of the court toward the Mass and the crucifix.

For example, on Good Friday, during Mass, probably just a couple of months after Calvin's departure, a French singer named Jehannet, who had been employed by the duke because of his talents regardless of his religious convictions, blatantly refused to kneel before the crucifix and defiantly exited the church. Apparently (according to an account by the duke), this came to the attention of the local inquisitor, who demanded an investigation of the court, where he found several other heretics.

The story, however, had an unexpected and humiliating twist for the duke, as all the accused refused to be subject to local authorities (under Ercole's supervision) and demanded to be judged directly by a papal council in Rome. While Ercole continued to hold them prisoners, Renée immediately wrote letters to King Francis, Marguerite, France's Grand-Master, the French ambassador in Venice, and even the pope.

The event soon developed into a major political controversy. Interestingly, both King Francis and the papal *nuncio* interpreted Ercole's action as an attempt to diminish France's influence on Ferrara. The suspicion was not unjustified, as Ercole had been able to live peaceably with most of the French members of his court until the recent treaties involving France. To many, the religious factors just seemed like a convenient excuse for Ercole to provoke or punish that country.

What followed was a time of political tug-of-war, as King Francis demanded that the accused be released to French authorities to be tried in their own country, while the pope insisted that, as this was a religious matter, they should be tried in Rome or by the inquisitor in Bologna, a city within the Papal States. Finally, due to disagreements among the papal *curia*, the prisoners were moved to Venice into the hands of the French ambassador, who in turn set them free.

Rome's final unexpected support of the French government in this matter worried and further humiliated the duke, who was beginning to feel his inadequacy to maintain in his duchy the same political stability his ancestors had painfully achieved and his father had fiercely defended. His policy toward Protestants, however, remained the same. They were tolerated unless they posed a risk to his political interests.

Ercole's policy of religious tolerance, in fact, had always included anyone who was profitable to his rule, including the Jews, who were at that time rejected and in some cases persecuted. Recognizing their great contribution to the prosperity of the city, Ercole allowed them to operate in peace, to the point that Ferrara hosted one of the largest Jewish communities in Europe.

Likewise, Protestant thinking had, by that time, seeped into every university in Italy and the *intelligentia*, so desirable for the enrichment of every court, was deeply drawn toward Reformed ideals. Ercole just could not create within the walls of his palace the cultural atmosphere that the Este had always proudly displayed — rivalling, in that sense, other powerful Renaissance families such as the Medici or the Sforza — without accepting dissident religious views.

In May 1537, for example, he warmly welcomed at his court poetess Vittoria Colonna (1490–1547), marchioness of Pescara (now mostly famous as correspondent of Michelangelo), who had come to Ferrara to introduce the renowned preacher Fra' Bernardino Ochino (1487–1564) and to find support for the establishment of his order of Capuchins in that city. Frail and emaciated by the rigorous habits of this order — an offshoot of the Observant Franciscans, whom they surpassed in devotion to a poor and austere life — Ochino was almost venerated by most Italians. His preaching was sweet but direct in denouncing the evils of the time, and full of references to the doctrine of justification by faith alone. Ercole was also immediately charmed by the friar and readily agreed to help in the foundation of his new convent.

A wolf in shepherd's clothing

According to the editors of the Latin edition of Calvin's epistles (*Calvini Epistolae*), Colonna brought to Ferrara a French Augustinian monk and renowned preacher named François Richardot (1507–1574), an exile from France, where his teachings were considered heretical. Others believe that Richardot had come to the Este court in 1535. In any case, Renée employed him as her adviser, almoner,[1] and occasional preacher. Richardot is important to our story because his bad advice — and the fact that Renée readily followed it — prompted Calvin to write his first and longest letter to the duchess.

Calvin had most likely met Richardot in Paris, where both men had studied around the same time, and knew his compromising tendencies quite well. In Ferrara, these tendencies became particularly evident when Richardot assured the duchess that it was perfectly legitimate to attend

both the Mass and the Lord's Supper. After all, he taught,
God looks at the heart.

Apparently, at least one of Renée's maids-of-honour knew
better. She remembered Calvin's teachings and, seeing a
sharp contrast between them and Renée's practice, refused
to follow Richardot's advice. Encouraged by the preacher,
Renée sternly reprimanded the lady and admonished the
rest of her court not to fall into the same mistake, which, in
her view, was causing unnecessary offence to other believers.

The news reached Calvin's ears when someone travelling
through Geneva mentioned this incident. Some believe it
may have been Anne de Parthenay (or de Pons), daughter
of Madame de Soubise, and that her report to Calvin was
one of the reasons why she and her husband were sent away
by the already suspicious duke in 1544. Others think it was
Françoise de Boussiron, another young noblewoman who
remained in contact with Calvin throughout her life.

Calvin's response does not bear a date, but several references
within the text lead us to believe that it was written in the
summer of 1537, during his first stay in Geneva. John Sinapius
(1505–1560), Renée's physician, had passed through Geneva
around that time, and it is possible that he brought back the
letter with him upon his return to Ferrara. Ercole, in fact,
was regularly intercepting Renée's correspondence, and
Calvin's letter could not be trusted to a regular messenger.

Calvin started this rather lengthy letter to Renée, the first in
our possession, with an apology for his boldness in sending
his unsolicited advice. He then gave some reasons for this

boldness, which help us to understand at least in part why he kept corresponding with Renée until his death. He felt compelled to write, he explained, not only out of concern for her well-being, which in his view would have been sufficient, but also because of her position as French princess and Italian duchess. 'It seems to me that all we who are called by the Lord in his goodness to be ministers of his holy Word must particularly care to do everything in our power for you, who can promote the kingdom of Jesus Christ more than common people and cause it to advance,' he said.

There was, however, something more, which distinguished Renée from many other rulers of their time. Calvin had seen in her some compelling marks of the work of God's Spirit. 'I have observed in you such fear of God and faithful disposition to obey him,' he explained, 'that, even without considering the high rank he has given you among men, I have been able to appreciate the virtues he has conferred on you and would consider myself accursed if I did not take advantage of these opportunities to serve you.' Besides, he had learned from Anne de Parthenay how Renée was eager to receive advice in these matters, since the many pressures at court had caused her much confusion, impairing her ability to make sound decisions.

Above all, Calvin was motivated by his great love for the truth. 'What moves me to speak is that I cannot tolerate that the Word of God is in such a way concealed, perverted, corrupted, and depraved before you regarding essential matters, by those whom you have graced with your trust and the endowment of authority,' he said. It was this love for the truth that compelled him to write a strong warning against Richardot. 'I know, Madame, that Christians should not denigrate their neighbour, and this has not been my intention,' he explained. 'However, if we see a wolf scattering the flock by appearing and acting as a shepherd, our Lord does not expect that we remain silent for fear of speaking ill of him.'

Calvin hesitated to go to great lengths in denouncing the perniciousness of the Roman Catholic Mass. He was sure that Renée was already fully acquainted with that subject and realized that a personal letter did not allow him enough space to cover such a weighty matter. He mentioned it however 'briefly' in a couple of paragraphs, showing that the Mass is in fact an act of blasphemy and idolatry as it claims to repeat Christ's sacrifice by human means.

The bulk of the letter answered a few possible objections by any who might claim that Christians could make a secret profession of faith in the heart without having to demonstrate it openly, particularly when, by such profession, they risked offending some weaker believers. This last objection was Richardot's excuse for encouraging attendance at both Catholic and Protestant rites, and Calvin rebutted it by clarifying that Christian liberty cannot be taken as a justification for breaking God's expressed commandments.

Calvin's pastoral heart is especially manifested at the closing of this letter, where he reminded Renée of the right motivation for her obedience to God. 'Therefore Madame,' he concluded, 'to whom God has given in his infinite mercy the knowledge of his name, enlightening you in the truth of his holy Gospel, you are to fulfil your vocation.' As Paul does in his letters, Calvin called Renée's attention to the great salvation and new life in Christ which God had provided for her, pointing out why Christians should ever want to obey him: not 'for fear that the Lord may punish us for our ungrateful behaviour,' but out of thankfulness for what he has done, letting God's Spirit and truth bring fruit in our hearts and transform us. 'I am not saying this so that you may do what you are not yet doing,' he wrote, 'but so that the work God has begun in you may be confirmed, day after day.'

Together with this epistle, Calvin sent another letter and a short booklet where he explained these matters more thoroughly. Since most of Renée's letters were destroyed, we do not know how she responded. We know that she kept Richardot at her service until 1544, and kept attending Mass during that period. On the other hand, from the fact that there is no record of further complaints from other Christians in her service, there is good reason to believe that she heeded Calvin's advice at least in part.[2]

3

MOTHER, PATRONESS

AND FRIEND

Even the stable keepers of Her Excellency speak very
comfortably of matters pertaining to the Scriptures
(A contemporary of Renée).

Renée as mother

By the end of 1538, all of Renée's five children were born
— Anna (1531–1607), Alfonso (1533–1597), Lucrezia
(1535–1598), Leonora (1537–1581) and Luigi (1538–1586).
They were for a while a deep source of comfort to her. She
must have often remembered Marot's prediction in the
poem he recited after her wedding, where the 'cruel night'
of the nuptials, when she was torn from her parents' arms by
the young duke, became sweet with the birth of her children.

The children's education was a common and heart-felt
interest for both Renée and Ercole, who provided them with

the best teachers available. A fan of the theatre, Ercole also made sure that the children were trained to act and dance for their guests. Their most impressive recitals included the *Andria* and the *Adelphi*, two comedies by Terence (195/185–159 BC), which they performed with great mastery in the original Latin at a very young age. The latter of these, the *Adelphi*, was a great success when performed in 1543 for Pope Paul III (1468–1549) during his visit to Ferrara, bringing on heavy applauses as all the children excelled in their roles.

All very beautiful and intelligent, the children also shone in all academic subjects, especially the girls. At eight years of age, Anna showed early signs of exceptional disposition in her studies, so much that Renée invited another young girl, Olympia Morata (1526–1555), to live at court as her tutor and companion. Olympia's official title was *fille du corps*, a little higher than *fille du chambre*. *Filles du corps* were usually employed without financial remuneration, but all their expenses, including fine clothing and books, were amply met.

Olympia, five years older than Anna, was already becoming famous for her prowess in classical studies. Under the tutelage of her father, humanist Fulvio Pellegrino Morato (*c.* 1483–1548), and other renowned professors, she had blossomed from a child prodigy to a young scholar, well versed in classical Latin and Greek and fully devoted to her studies.

Fulvio Morato was not unknown at the court of Este, where he had worked as a tutor in the past. He had been forced to leave in 1532, presumably by some disagreements with Duke Alfonso, and had moved to nearby Vicenza, where he had founded what some called 'a true Calvinist school'. He was the author of some academic books, as well a very popular treatise on the meaning of colours and flowers, which had become a best-seller, especially among the ladies.

We do not know what brought Morato back to Ferrara, but his return coincided with his readmission to court, his employment at the University of Ferrara, and the invitation for Olympia to live at the court of Este. It was not unusual for young people to live under the patronage of nobility. Lesser families, in fact, often sent their teenage children to the courts of higher lords to work as squires or dames and learn, in the process, the arts of court society. At court, these young people received optimal educations, and the boys had a chance to get acquainted with the arts of war, while the women learned all the qualities and skills that would make them good marital prospects. Besides, at court they all had a chance to become known and appreciated by visiting families, increasing their chances for career or marriage.

For Olympia, however, things were somewhat different. She was not entering the court of Este as a dame, but as a tutor for Anna, and her own education was restricted to the humanistic subjects in which she had already excelled. Her teachers discouraged her from wasting her time with 'womanly' tasks such as embroidery and weaving, and she did not mind at all, because literary studies were her passion. At court, Olympia gave a few dissertations on Cicero, a classical author she had come to love, defending him against some recent critics. Her fame rapidly increased.

Eager to show the magnificence of their court, where such a higher education was afforded to women, the duke and duchess scheduled more public discourses for Olympia, who continued to revel in their praises.

Olympia and Anna became close friends, sharing the same passion for studies. One project they probably mastered together was the translation from Italian vernacular into Latin of the first two tales of Giovanni Boccaccio (1313–1375), vivid social parodies of the vices and decay of the Roman Church. Naturally, Renée made sure that the study of theology was a large part of her daughter's education, providing her with free access to the Scriptures in the Greek Septuagint (the version Olympia preferred), the Latin Vulgate, and the Italian translation by Antonio Brucioli (*c.* 1495–1566), as well as to a large library of treatises and commentaries.

Renée's second child, Alfonso, received an education fit for a prince, under Ercole's proud and watchful eye. Father and son spent much time together, often hunting in the family game reserves. He was an adventurous and independent son, and his repeated escapes to France in later life prove that he never changed.

The duchess oversaw carefully the instruction of her other two daughters, Lucrezia and Leonora, also very studious and gifted, but her last child, Luigi, was by tradition destined to an ecclesiastical career within the Roman Catholic Church and educated accordingly. It was in the year of his birth, in fact, that Ercole's brother Ippolito became cardinal and promised to take Luigi under his patronage.

The fact that Renée had no more children after Luigi gave rise to rumours that Ercole had sexual relations with his wife only in order to obtain what he wanted — a heir for his duchy and, as was customary with nobility, a representative of his family within the Catholic church (for prestige, political gain, and perhaps some favour from heaven). Many other rumours circulated about their marriage, particularly about Ercole's extra-marital relationships (not unusual in the courts of nobility at that time). We have, however, no absolute proof that any of this was true.

Renée as friend

Still, in the midst of a troubled marriage and difficult situation, we have glimpses of Renée as a joyous young woman who enjoyed life and friendship. We find her riding in her large estates, playing tennis, especially in its earlier form of *jeu de paume* (with a glove instead of a racket) and enjoying ball-room dances with her ladies-in-waiting. A typical week, as we read in one of her letters, included a dinner with a cardinal and her husband, a picnic in the woods with Ercole and a bishop, and a visit to a relative.

As customary for a ruler's wife, she led her ladies in performing all the traditional tasks of charity and distribution of alms, which included the public function of washing the feet of the city's poor on Holy Thursday.

We know that she loved plants and trees and personally oversaw their care in the large gardens of the palace, sharing with the Este family a passion for rare and exotic plants. In a serious letter written to her husband, we find that she had just picked some fresh grapes from her vineyards and was about to send him some fruits imported by her gardener from Naples.

In spite of the loss of most of her letters, we notice in what is left her very close ties to her friends. In particular, after the departure of Madame de Soubise, we recognize a tight friendship between Renée and both Anne de Parthenay and her husband, Antoine de Pons, a childhood friend who was now her *chevallier d'honneur.* One long letter by her to Antoine while he was in France on a mission provides us with an image of Renée's daily life at that time. Later authors have tried to attach some rumours to this letter, but there is no proof that Renée's relationship with Antoine went beyond a simple friendship.

'If this letter is badly written,' she said, 'it is because I am writing it in bed, and it is early morning. [...] Your little dog came to give me a thousand caresses between the covers. He took the pen from my hand with his little mouth, then came to lie down, with my arm and palm of my hand under his head, and slept. So I did too, just to keep him company. I do not know which of us needed it more.' In a second letter, she described another time when the little dog came to sleep on her arm. 'When I tried to move him,' she said, 'he acted all cute and kissed me as if to say, "do not do it".'

The more Renée loved Anne and Antoine, however, the more Ercole detested them, particularly Anne, whom he considered worse than her mother and responsible for the continued influx of Protestants at court. In 1544, he accused both Anne and Antoine of treason and of plotting against his life and sent them back to France.

Renée as patroness

Renée exercised her role of ruler over her court carefully. She sought the well-being of her subjects, tended generously to their needs, oversaw events, dinners, and parties, provided advice in the process of courtship and marital relations, paid generous dowries to her ladies, rejoiced over the birth of babies and provided the best education for all. Like other female rulers of her time, she also became a patroness of artists, poets, and musicians, contributing with frequent concerts, yearly literary contests, and other cultural events, to the fame of Ferrara as a vibrant intellectual centre and creative haven for masters such as Ludovico Ariosto (1474–1533) and Titian (*c.* 1490–1576).

Her court was run according to French standards. Her financial records, a great source of information on what was bought and given, followed the same system of computation as those of the French royal court. Her quarters were also autonomous and structured on the French model, with bedrooms, a chapel, and various utility rooms, such as a bakery, a wine cellar, a kitchen, and a stable.

Mostly, however, she is famous as patroness of banned or endangered Protestants, who were often employed in her service in different capacities. Her piety and generosity were sung by many. Marot described her court as a point of gathering for 'all children of virtue', who were 'brothers and

sisters in the truth'. Several Protestant works of that time
included obsequious dedications to her as one most able to
discern and appreciate religious writings.

In 1540, she received from Ercole a villa in Consandolo, a
humid region in the delta of the Po River, fifty miles southeast of Ferrara. With this gift, Ercole may have hoped, at
least partially, to keep his consort hidden from the watchful
eye of the Roman curia, sparing himself questions and
embarrassment. Around that time, in fact, papal authorities
had begun to tighten their measures against Protestants and
were putting pressure on the duke to do likewise.

Even today, few people realize that Italy had been for
quite some time a fertile and eager breeding ground for
Reformed doctrines. Luther's doctrines were circulating
widely, both by writings and by word of mouth. Some
orders, such as the Augustinians, the Franciscans, and the
Capuchins, recognized in his teachings the pure dogmas
of their founders and of the church fathers, and began to
incorporate them, albeit subtly, in their sermons. Even many
church officials were convinced of the truth of the Reformed
creeds and were hoping and praying for a change within the
Church of Rome.

Books were imported from Germany, translated, and repro-
duced, mostly in Venice, a city just north-east of Ferrara. According to some scholars, in fact, Venice's clandestine network
for the diffusion of Protestant literature was without equal in
Europe.[1] We know that Renée had close ties with Venetian
printers, financing the production of Bibles and other religious books, not only in Italian but in other languages.

Besides Ferrara, several Italian cities, particularly Naples, Lucca, and Modena, saw the rise of small but vibrant Protestant communities. It is no wonder that the Church of Rome was worried. Dreading the alarming prospect of losing ground in its own territory, in 1542, after a disappointing attempt — doomed to defeat from the start — to find conciliation with Protestants at the Diet of Regensburg, the Church tightened its measures of repression. It was then that it re-established, among other things, the Roman inquisition as supreme tribunal in religious matters. For Ercole, this meant that Rome had greater authority over him in matters of religion and heresy.

Renée must have accepted the villa in Consandolo with relief. In spite of the inclement weather, she enjoyed more freedom there to invite and host whomever she liked, building a large library of Reformed books and treatises, and enjoying the preaching of Protestant ministers, so much that a visitor to the villa stated, 'Even the stable keepers of Her Excellency speak very comfortably of matters pertaining to the Scriptures.'

4

MOUNTING PERSECUTION

*Indeed, the hour is coming when whoever kills you
will think he is offering service to God*
(John 16:2).

Renée rode the wave of renewed persecution well, helping
several Italian Protestants to flee beyond the Alps, and
turning the papal decree to her advantage. In 1543, when
Pope Paul III visited Ferrara, she asked him personally to
withdraw her from the jurisdiction of local inquisitors and
to place her under the sole control of the church in Rome.
Evidently, she believed that a distant enemy is always
preferable to one at the gate. Besides, she knew the pettiness
of local inquisitors too well and their burning desire to reveal
and crush her involvement with the Protestant movement.

The lengthy case of Fanino Fanini

While it is difficult to determine the effects of the newly-established inquisition on the duchy of Ferrara, it is true that the following years saw a rise in the number of arrests and trials of heretics within its borders. The most famous case was that of Fanino Fanini (1520–1550) a well-known baker who was arrested in 1547 for having embraced and spread Reformed doctrines. Moved by the tears and persuasion of his wife, sister, and children, he eventually recanted and was freed, only to discover that he could no longer live with himself, so he asked God for forgiveness and resumed his work of propagation of the gospel more fervently than ever.

He was finally arrested again in February 1549 when he visited, together with four friends, a convent of nuns, familiarizing them so well with the Reformed teachings that, when questioned, the sisters openly called themselves 'Lutherans'. Fanini was imprisoned in Ferrara, where Ercole laboured to obtain the right to set a trial according to his own terms and by a tribunal including local as well as papal representatives. The negotiations continued for months until, in September 1549, Fanini was tried in Ferrara and condemned to die. The harsh sentence (the first death sentence for matters of heresy in Ferrara) was probably sought by the duke to prove that he could handle problems with enough firmness and determination, precluding the need for papal intervention in every case.

The sentence, however, caused a loud outcry, as several personalities pleaded with the duke to change his mind.

These included Olympia Morata, who had been dismissed from court, her friend Lavinia della Rovere, and Lavinia's father-in-law, Camillo Orsini (1530–1580), a well-known military captain who offered to take Fanini under his care, becoming personally responsible for his behaviour. Renée joined the pleadings, sending heart-felt letters to her husband and appealing to his generosity and proven concern for the poor.

Once again, Ercole had to weigh his moves. He still had the power to forgive Fanini or at least to turn his sentence into a lesser punishment. An act of mercy would have emphasized his magnanimity among the people, as his suitors were reminding him. At this point, however, he decided that showing an iron hand to the Pope was more important than gaining the praise of his subjects. Pope Paul III's death in November 1549 created a standstill in the situation, sustaining the hopes of Fanini's supporters, as Ercole waited for the election of a new pope. In August 1550, six months after the appointment of Pope Julius III (1487–1555), Fanini was hung. Then, as was customary in the case of heresy, his body was burned and the ashes were cast into the Po River.

The puzzling rejection of Olympia Morata

The dismissal of Olympia from court shortly before Fanini's trial raises some unanswered questions. In 1547, after eight years of faithful service at court, she went home to spend some time with her father, who was seriously ill. It was supposed to be a short visit, and both Renée and Anna encouraged her to return soon. Morato's fluctuating state of health kept her longer than foreseen, until the following year, when he died.

At that point, her job at court took on a new significance. It was no longer just a task she loved to do, which brought her satisfaction and fame. It had become an urgent necessity. Her mother was now a widow and her position was important for the sustenance of the family. Her sisters were all hoping to find good positions in some noble families and were in need of Olympia's mediation. However, when Olympia returned to court, she was told that she was no longer needed.

There is some logic to that crushing revelation. Olympia had originally come to court as a tutor and companion for Anna, who in 1548 was given in marriage to Duke Francis of Guise (1519–1563) and moved to France. From that point of view, her services were no longer necessary. It is difficult, though, to understand why Renée, who was generally known for her prodigality in helping the poor and the outcast, made no effort to take Olympia back or at least to assist her family. In fact, she apparently cut all ties with the Moratos, precluding any possibility of Olympia's siblings finding places at her court.

This puzzling question has raised many suppositions. In one of her letters, Olympia talks of 'the hatred and slander of certain evil people'. We do not know who these people may have been or what the slander was, but the main suspect has traditionally been Jérôme Bolsec (d. 1584), an ex-Carmelite friar who had spent some time in Geneva, where he had some disagreements with Calvin on the doctrine of predestination. Renée had employed him as almoner, but some say that Ercole had used him to spy on his wife.

Olympia's judgment of the situation and of Renée maintained over the years a tinge of embitterment, although she clearly recognized the hand of God's providence, which eventually brought good fruit in her life. In a letter written two years after her rejection, she said, 'I was immediately abandoned by my lady and received only in the most humiliating manner.'

On the other hand, although Renée's silence and apparent indifference toward Olympia appear puzzling, it seems that she did not completely forget the young scholar. In fact, on the occasion of her wedding to Andreas Grunthler (d. 1555) at the end of 1549 or beginning of 1550, she provided her with a dowry of 500 *livres*, more than the usual 200- or 300-*livres* dowries she paid for ladies of this rank. Grunthler, a medical student with a vast classical education and a flair for poetry and music, worked in Renée's court as a tutor for Lucrezia and Leonora until September 1548, and it is possible that Renée (who was involved, like most rulers, in her subjects' personal lives) was informed of his love for Olympia.

Any attempt to understand Renée's thoughts toward Olympia at this time is, however, nothing but guess-work. The answer could be a combination of several explanations. Olympia had outlived her usefulness at court; and maybe some rumours had been spread at the same time. What we know is that it was a difficult time for the duchess. On the one hand, her daughter Anna had just left for France to marry a member of the Guise family, staunch defenders of the Roman Catholic Church. At home, she had just begun to realize that her request to be judged directly by the Roman curia was not as clever as she might have thought.

The religious tribunal in Rome, in fact, unlike local inquisitors, had the ability to collect and compare the results of many court trials. By 1548, these results had unmistakably shown that Renée was not just a charitable woman giving some respite to French fugitives, but that she had harboured many suspected heretics and that her court was a breeding ground for new and dangerous opinions.

Heightened suspicions

By 1550, around the same time as Fanini's execution, church officials openly confronted the duke with their strong suspicions of Renée's activities. There were warnings that she was now living 'as a Lutheran'.[1] Among many others, the Este ambassador to Rome had reported to Ercole, 'They believe Her Excellency to be fully Lutheran, from what they have seen in many court trials held here against many who were held on similar accounts, and that not only the men, but the women have been asserting these new opinions more affirmatively than even Bucer or Melanchthon. They also spread slanders, saying that during the Holy week all her courtiers eat meat in public, which here is considered a great scandal, even if few lords keep Lent, but rather eat privately.'

The church's suspicions were, of course, not unfounded. Around that time, Renée had abandoned some of her customary caution. After some continued correspondence not only with Calvin, but with other ministers in Switzerland, she received the clandestine visit of one of them, Giulio della Rovere (1504–1581), who preached fifteen sermons to her court, greatly strengthening their convictions and their faith. Two years later, Della Rovere wrote a treatise, *Exhortation to Martyrdom*, which was meant as a response to many questions that were troubling Italian Protestants at that time.

By then, it had become evident that Italian Protestants could no longer straddle a fence or hide their convictions in the hope that the Roman Catholic Church would recognize and abandon its errors. The repeated failure of conciliation attempts (the Council of Trent had openly condemned the doctrine of justification by faith alone in 1547) and the consequent iron hand of the Inquisition had clearly shown that there were only two ethical choices for a Christian: leave the country or be willing to face death. Della Rovere exhorted believers to choose the second option, even if his experience had been quite different. Arrested in 1541 for openly preaching justification by faith alone, he was forced to recant, but later escaped to Switzerland, where he fully embraced his faith and subsequently pastored two churches.

Even though Della Rovere's sermons were mild (a visitor commented that they could have been preached in front of the Pope), they had a noticeable effect on Renée. It was around this time, in fact, that she made a final commitment to stop attending Mass, switching to the sacrament of the Lord's Supper, celebrated in simple obedience to Christ with flat homemade bread and wine, without mention of transubstantiation, or of renewal of Jesus' sacrifice. In 1551, Italian Reformer Pier Paolo Vergerio (1498–1565) commented, 'The Duchess of Ferrara was still attached to the mass (!),[2] causing great offence and sorrow to the faithful, but recently she has publicly freed and cleansed herself, with our great joy.'

The same year, in fact, we see Renée attending the Lord's Supper during the visit of Isabella Bresegna (*c.* 1510–1567) a Reformed noblewoman of Spanish descent who spent several months in Consandolo with her son and daughter-in-law, outwardly to consult Renée's physician,[3] but secretly to spend time in a Protestant community. Out of caution, the Protestant Lord's Supper was normally celebrated in the privacy of Renée's quarters, with only a dozen of her most trusted courtiers.

There were, however, other aspects of Renée's behaviour which seemed troubling to visitors such as Della Rovere, particularly her lack of discernment in offering aid and support. While, on the one hand, her generosity seemed commendable, Della Rovere sensed or feared in the duchess an inability or unwillingness to distinguish between scriptural and unscriptural teachings. Particularly upsetting to him, as to many other Reformers, were the teachings of Giorgio Siculo, a former monk who was considered heretical by both Catholics and Protestants. Siculo taught, among other things, that men have full ability to act according to God's law and can therefore be saved by their own merits. This was basically the same doctrine taught by Pelagius (*c.* 354–420/440) and firmly repudiated by Augustine (354–

430) and by later church councils. Siculo claimed that God had revealed to him personally the truth of this position.

In spite of Renée's help and protection, the Roman Church finally captured Siculo and executed him on 23 May 1551. The day after his execution, Della Rovere wrote Renée a letter to warn her against Siculo's error and other unscriptural doctrines taught by some of her protégés. We do not know how she reacted, but the composition of her court leads us to think that she continued to help anyone who asked, regardless of their religious convictions.

5

FIERY TRIALS

Beloved, do not be surprised at the fiery trial
when it comes upon you to test you
(1 Peter 4:12).

Ercole takes action

Ercole continued to respond to warnings about his wife with feigned surprise and repeated promises. Soon, however, the need for intervention became obvious. He could not afford to be seen as a man who could not rule over his own house; otherwise, how could he rule over his duchy? Besides, any doubt about his court's conformity to Roman Catholic orthodoxy was an open invitation to investigations and trouble.

Acting against his wife was not simple. She was still under the protection of the King of France and judicially under the jurisdiction of papal authorities. He therefore decided to deal with the problem indirectly, by weakening her support. Slowly, he started to reduce the size of her court, by eliminating those who raised most suspicions.

In August 1552, we find reports that Renée had complained to the new king of France, Henry II (1519–1559), about the way the duke had been treating her, expressing her desire to return to France with her daughters. In fact, she even consulted other people on the possibility of leaving her husband.

It was then that she received the visit of another pastor, Paolo Gaddi, who had studied in Geneva under Calvin. On this matter, Gaddi suggested that she ask for the Reformer's advice. Apparently, Renée accepted the suggestion gladly, but kept postponing. In a letter to Calvin, Gaddi suggests as a possible cause of this procrastination the poor advisers she had around her. 'She has run up against some terrible counsellors who cannot be sent away,' he wrote Calvin. 'Besides, she lacks a faithful minister of God's Word, able to exhort her and to keep the seed from being choked by brambles and thorns.'

We do not know who the 'terrible counsellors' might have been. The fact that they could not be expelled suggests that they might have been appointed to her court by the duke. From a letter written by Calvin to the Reformer Heinrich Bullinger (1504–1575) the following year, it seems that he had never received a letter from Renée after Gaddi's message, and was concerned that her missives might have been intercepted or lost. Finally, the same year, Calvin received a message from the duchess, but it was just a practical request asking him if he could find two girls willing to work at her court as *filles du corps*. As strange as the request may seem to us today, Renée was concerned that they were honest, hardworking, and not prone to gossip, and she knew that Calvin would give her the best recommendation.

In the meantime, a dreadful scenario was developing in Ferrara, one that Renée was not yet foreseeing. A Jesuit father, Jean Pelletier, who had directed a college of Jesuits in Rome, had arrived in the city in 1551 with the expressed desire of starting a similar institution. In reality, he had been sent to spy on the duchess. Carefully, he spent a few years studying the situation, until in the spring of 1554 he found the perfect opportunity to strike, and seized it. At a time when the duke was feeling especially pressured by the papal authorities and appalled by his wife's open refusal to attend the Easter Mass with her daughters, Pelletier proposed a seven-step plan on how to rid his court of heretics.

The steps were as follows:

1. Expel any suspected persons, especially the most influential ones: the preacher, the almoner, and the daughter's Greek teacher, all heretics;
2. Say Mass every day at her house;
3. Make sure that everyone has a rosary and recites it, together with other customary prayers to Mary;
4. Expel the women, especially the most influential ones;
5. Allow only preachers who are licensed by the duke and only at times prescribed by him;
6. Bring Madame closer to the palace so she can gain more fear and respect;
7. At this point, the door will be open for the duke to do what his conscience tells him to do.

This plan was obviously conceived with the specific goal of isolating the duchess and giving her some doctrinal instruction, in the hope that she would return to the Roman Catholic faith. It was not meant as a general rule in every case. Her Protestants retinue, in fact, was simply expelled, and no one was captured and questioned at this time.

Ercole embraced the plan whole-heartedly, as a godsend not only to solve his immediate problems with his wife and the annoying papal authorities, but also to set his duchy in step with the current political situation. In England, in fact, the Roman Catholic Queen Mary I (1516–1558) was planning a marriage with Philip II of Spain (1527–1598), and their projected union, together with the atmosphere of full counter-reformation in Italy and Spain, was changing the face of Europe. Promptly, he proclaimed a decree that all heretics and heresies would be banned from his duchy.

In an effort to keep good relations with the King of France, Ercole wrote him a letter explaining the situation and asking him to send a good Roman Catholic theologian to help his poor wife and her daughters to free themselves from the strong misconceptions they had been taught by ill-intentioned persons. King Henry II complied, sending Matthieu Ory (1492–1557), a French theologian and inquisitor, prior of the Dominican order, with the intention of converting the duchess without creating a scandal.

A counter-attack

At that time, Léon Jamet, who had been in France since 1548, taking care of Renée's interests there, rushed to

Geneva to inform Calvin of the situation. The ambassador for Ferrara in Paris wrote that he was sent by the Guises (maybe by Anna, who had married into that family) to scare the duchess, explaining the consequences of her resistance. By stopping in Geneva, Jamet showed his true intentions.

Calvin reacted promptly, by sending to Renée, within a couple of weeks, François de Morel, a French pastor then serving in Geneva. In the accompanying letter, he shared his heart-felt and sincere concern for Renée, and told her how much he would have preferred to go to her in person. Sadly, he was not able to leave his duties at that time. He asked her then to receive Morel as sent not by him, 'but by God', listing his many qualities and adding that, being a nobleman by birth, he would know how to fit well in her court without raising suspicions.

The greatest proof of Morel's loyalty and dedication was however, in Calvin's eyes, his readiness to go to serve the duchess in spite of the obvious dangers. 'You can judge by yourself, Madame, the righteous zeal and devotion he is showing in serving you by the fact that, from the start, he has preferred to partake of your cross and to suffer with you in this time of need, rather than waiting for the end of these troubles. Because of this, he needs no further recommendations.'

1554 was a difficult year for Calvin. Much had changed in his life since his visit to Renée in 1536. After leaving her court, he had been persuaded to help the church in Geneva, where he was met with much contempt, criticism, and spite. His conviction that the church of Christ must be disciplined and subject to leadership and well-defined rules, including excommunication for those who refused to comply, provoked the anger of many citizens and eventually, in 1538, led to his expulsion from the city.

Less than three years later, however, the Genevans realized that they could not organize and sustain a stable church without him and called him back from Strasbourg, where he had lived happily for some time. Convinced by his friends that God wanted him to heed the call, Calvin returned hesitantly to the place where he had been so terribly mistreated, and worked once again for the good of the church. The welcome back had not been, however, unanimous. Calvin still had many enemies and both 1553 and 1554 brought many problems, mostly related again to church discipline. He just could not leave the church at that time.

The fact that he considered going to Ferrara, especially at such a dangerous time, to strengthen and comfort Renée, speaks volumes about his opinion of the duchess. In spite of her wavering, he held to the commitment he had expressed in his first letter to her. Sending Morel was a further proof of this commitment, as pastors were very scarce at that time.

Weakness in crisis

Ory arrived in Ferrara in July 1554, one month before Morel. At first, his talks with Renée did not seem successful. Finally, he threatened her by saying that all her lands would be taken away from her if she did not return to the religion of Rome. She had, in fact, several lands in France still in her name and undoubtedly wanted to keep them as a refuge for the future. This threat seemed to have some effect, because on 7 September, the Florentine ambassador to Ferrara reported to his lord that Renée had started to attend Mass again.

His letter, however, ended with a dramatic statement: 'P.S. Last night Madame was imprisoned in the duke's palace, and no one can speak to her. She has only two women in her company, and those who went to take her from her house at midnight say that she was very cheerful. The daughters are in a monastery.'

Why such sudden and drastic measures? After all, Renée seemed to be slowly complying. According to Pelletier, the catalyst was the discovery of Morel. 'This was caused by treason by the enemies of our holy faith, who have sent from Geneva a count or marquis. [...] This traitor has come in incognito and has spent up to six hours per night preaching and sowing tares, persuading them to persevere and to eat meat as usual, whereas it had already been removed.' The duke acted promptly, the same night.

As soon as Renée and her daughters were removed and everyone else expelled, the guards, following the duke's orders, searched the villa and confiscated all the books. 'They found about one hundred of them,' Pelletier continued, 'the most troubling anyone could imagine, and took them.' Others reported that the guards also retrieved 'infinite letters' from various European Reformers, prompting the comment, 'with many letters, she provides preachers for the whole State'. If one hundred books seem relatively few today, it was an impressive number at that time, when the largest book collections owned by noblewomen reached at most thirty titles. Over the years, we know from the financial records that Renée bought at least 160 books, and many more were given to her as presents.

Renée's daughters were taken to the Corpus Christi monastery in Modena, about 35 miles from Ferrara. Throughout the ordeal, Ercole's only message to Renée was, *Et sub viri potestate eris* ('You shall be under the rule of man'), to which Renée reportedly answered, 'My lord, you are lord over my body but not over my soul.'

While Renée was detained in her room in the palace, Ory visited her daily, insisting that she return to the doctrines of the Roman Catholic Church. Initially she stood firm, until, after a few days of pleading, Ory announced that he would go back to France to report the news of her obstinacy to the king, warning her again that she would lose any claims she had in France.

The following hours were probably tormented for Renée. She had just cut herself off from the protection of the king of France, who had been her only earthly refuge all her life. Her future was set within the four walls of her room, without her daughters, without friends, without books, and without any contact with the outside world, except for daily disturbing visits by Pelletier and others who had joined him in this work of conversion: the Franciscan Dominique du Gabre (1547–1557), bishop of Lodève (who had also been at court since 1551), and the local inquisitor Fra Girolamo Papino, a favourite of the duke.

On the surface, the way around it seemed easy. She just had to attend Mass and verbally agree with her inquisitors, a choice that, after all, was pursued by many at that time. After much thought, at two in the morning, she finally called her steward and asked him to inquire if Ory was still in the castle's premises. If he was, the steward should ask him to stay and say Mass for her the next day. Ory was there, and Renée attended Mass, promising to confess her sins to a priest very soon. This was enough to appease Ory, who returned gladly to France, bearing good news of Renée's submission to the Church of Rome.

Both Pelletier and Ercole, however, still doubted her sincerity. As far as they were concerned, attending Mass was not enough. To regain her freedom, Renée had to reconcile herself fully with the Roman Catholic Church, attending confession, receiving the Eucharist, and exhibiting such a change of behaviour that everyone would know that she had understood her mistake and had recanted freely and not out of submission to her husband. Ercole also planned to oversee closely the choosing of her new courtiers and to limit (if not take away completely) her provisions.

Renée resisted a few more days. Finally, on 13 September, weakened by the barrage of threats and forced indoctrination, she capitulated, confessed her sins to Pelletier and partook of the Eucharist. According to the Jesuit, her confession lasted three hours, with strong repentance and tears. She also wrote a letter to her husband, promising complete submission. Fully satisfied, Pelletier wrote to Ignatius of Loyola (1491–1556), head of the Jesuits, taking credit for the successful conversion, and agreed that Renée's daughters should be returned to her.

After this, Pelletier worked hard to educate Renée and her daughters in the Roman Catholic faith. He gave them daily lessons and assigned them the reading of doctrinal and hagiographical books. For penance, he restricted his choices to the reciting of the rosary and litanies 'to support them in the prayers to the saints'. He insisted that Renée sit in church where she could be well visible by all and not in a corner as she did initially. He established that they would confess their sins to a priest and partake of the Eucharist four times a year: Easter, Christmas, and two more times which he reserved the right to determine as needed.

Around the same time, du Gabre reported having had a long talk with Renée, where he explained that she would not receive any more money from France and could only appeal to her husband's mercy. It was the final blow. Under those unforeseen circumstances, Renée asked him to intercede for her with Ercole, promising that she would stop financing heretics and allow him to see her ill-famed financial records. Apparently, in fact, besides her prodigal expenses on which the duke had always frowned, the duchess had a secret fund for the support of Protestants, and the donations from that fund were recorded as expenditures without mentioning the recipients.

Renée's final confession seemed appeasing to the duke, who was already quite taken up with other events, such as a war he had engaged against Florence and the humiliation of having his runaway son, Alfonso, shipped back to him from France, where he had gone some months earlier to live a life of debauchery at the king's expense.

6

The slow road back

*Our good God is always ready to receive us in his grace
and, when we fall, holds out his hand
that our falls may not be fatal*
(John Calvin).

What went wrong

We linger in surprise and disappointment as we turn this page in Renée's life. We want to know why, what thoughts crossed her mind, and we are frustrated by the lack of first-hand documents. We can only listen to the voices of those who were around her — mostly inquisitors or visitors.

The simplest explanation is that Renée might have felt justified in pretending to acquiesce to her inquisitors in order to regain her freedom. This attitude, strongly opposed by Calvin, was in fact widespread in those days. Even Marguerite of Navarre, who had exercised a considerable influence on Renée's life, had often conformed outwardly to the practices of the Roman Catholic Church, believing that only the inner convictions mattered.

There were other possible reasons. Pelletier, for example, had believed from his earliest conversations with Renée that bringing her back to the Roman fold would have been an easy task, given her poor theological knowledge. 'The poor woman has no education,' he wrote to Loyola. 'She only knows a few passages of Paul's letters in the vernacular, and even those are misinterpreted, and she has been preaching to me with her few chatters, but I always stopped her when she did not conform to the true light of the Gospel, laughing pleasantly with her. May God convert her. I believe it must be done.'

A description of Renée as an uneducated woman, particularly in theological matters, seems to clash with the great words of admiration she had received from Reformers who had come in contact with her in the past, but there may be several explanations. First of all, the fact that Pelletier was 'laughing pleasantly with her' leads us to think that this was a light conversation (he had also repeated the adverb 'pleasantly' referring to this conversation earlier in the letter), so Renée might have decided to avoid a serious discussion. Second, we know from the rest of Pelletier's correspondence with Loyola that he had been trying to persuade his superior of his complete ability to deal with this matter.

Some scholars, however, have wondered if his judgment may reveal some partial truth. Maybe Renée was not as theologically prepared as we would have expected, and maybe this was really her downfall. In spite of her large library of books and Bibles in French, Italian, Hebrew, Latin, and Greek, we know that she had very little personal guidance apart from her correspondence with Reformers abroad. As Della Rovere and Gaddi had lamented, she lacked faithful and constant pastoral direction. Instead, she kept surrounding herself with pseudo-Christians and outright heretical teachings (some of her protégés were anti-Trinitarian) which were bound to take their toll, creating confusion in her mind.

We also have, in this regard, a very puzzling statement by Olympia, who wrote that while she was at Renée's court she was never 'able to lift her eyes to anything high or divine — not even to read the books of either the Old or New Testament', and that she only 'returned to divine studies' after her estrangement. We cannot infer from her words that this was the general rule for anyone living with the duchess, since many others had found rest and spiritual encouragement under her protection. Clearly, Olympia was speaking about herself. In an effort to please her patrons, she had devoted herself completely to humanistic studies to the neglect of a serious and methodical study of God's Word. We see in other letters how much her thought had become influenced by the Epicureanism of ancient writers, especially Lucretius, who believed in a distant and indifferent deity.

On the other hand, this and other similar comments by Olympia shed some light on life at court and help us to understand another aspect of Renée's situation. Both in her *Dialogue between Lavinia della Rovere and Olympia Morata* (1550), and in her *Dialogue between Theophila and Philotima* (1551–52), Olympia talks about flatterers, rumours, and women riding around in gilded carriages, overly concerned about clothes. She talks about distractions and the lure of material things, until one of her characters makes a confession that is considered to be autobiographical: 'I too was stuck in the same mud and would still be if God in his mercy had not pulled me out.'

It is no wonder then that, around the end of her life, Olympia refused the offer to live in the castle of Heidelberg as a guest of the Elector Palatine. 'Not that I would wish to live at court again — that I could do here, but...' she wrote to her friend Anne of Este, ending with an eloquent pause.

The atmosphere in a Renaissance court, with its disruptions, intrigues, and impositions, could easily cause serious difficulties to those trying to stay true to their religious convictions, as Calvin reiterated in his comment upon receiving, two months later, the news of Renée's abjuration: 'What can I say but that an example of constancy is a rare thing among princes?'

'What can you do?' Theodore Beza (1519–1605), Calvin's right-hand man, asked resignedly. 'You have done your duty.'

Gradual recovery

Still, Calvin could not be silent. Even if Renée had not written to him, he sought the first feasible and safe chance to send her a letter of encouragement and comfort. He had to wait until February 1555, because he could not find the right messenger going that way. 'Since you have started to have problems,' he said, 'I have not been sure of whom to trust.'

Relying only on what he had heard, Calvin carefully talked about Renée's denial of her faith as a rumour not yet verified or a simple impression he had derived from the reports he had received. 'I think you had to leave the right way in order to please the world. In fact, if those who had waged with you such a relentless war to pull you away from God's service are now leaving you alone, this is a bad sign.'

His message was, however, full of hope: 'Besides, Madame, since our good God is always ready to receive us in his grace and, when we fall, holds out his hand that our falls may not be fatal, I entreat you to regain strength. If, through your weakness, the enemy has gotten this one time the better hand over you, may he not have the final victory, but may he know that those whom God has lifted again are doubly strengthened against any struggle.'

After directing her hope to God only, Calvin encouraged her to remember Christ's sacrifice and all its ensuing benefits, including the great promises of strength in our frailties, and to order not only her life, but her whole household, in order to stop all slanders against her.

Renée's recovery was slow, but sure. In June 1555, in a letter most probably (according to academic consensus) directed to her but generally addressed 'to a lady', Calvin regretted that she could not yet enjoy peace of mind in God's service, but rejoiced in knowing that she was still struggling and fighting in the effort to obey, because this struggle signalled the work of God's Spirit in her heart. With that certainty, he encouraged her again to look to God, knowing that he is the one who both begins and brings to completion our salvation.

'I trust God,' he wrote, 'that as he has impressed in your heart a special disposition to honour him, he will also increase and manifest the means of putting into practice the good will with which he has endowed you. Since it is his province to both begin and perfect his good work, we boldly hope in his power to save, which is meant to give evidence of his virtue.'

Soon, Renée managed to live relatively undisturbed, mostly in her villa in Consandolo, with her daughters and a new group of courtiers. As various interrogations proved, she was able to surround herself again with Protestants (some of whom had lived with her earlier) and to support the persecuted.

The relative calm she enjoyed at that time is apparent in an angry letter she wrote in September of the same year to the French ambassador in Venice, protesting at the arrest of her goldsmith, who had been taken from his bed in the middle of the night and imprisoned because he had answered a question about purgatory in a 'Lutheran' way. This letter shows that, by then, Renée believed she had the right to protect her court members from inquisitors' attacks.

In spite of warnings by Rome and other agents, Ercole limited his measures to a strict supervision of Renée's income (mostly from her lands in France) and a confiscation of her valuables, including jewels. This was probably a way to hit the duchess where it hurt most, by restraining her financial independence. It was also a measure aimed at ending her continual support of the Protestant cause.

Ercole's plans, however, were thwarted by a letter of Renée to King Henry II, where she persuaded him to defend her material assets as French property. Ercole conceded. At that time, France and Ferrara were once again trying to strengthen their alliance, and he could not jeopardize that relationship over some conjugal matters. However, he interpreted Renée's resistance as an act of retaliation against him for having prevented her from 'persevering in her heretical life'. In his view, she had no reason to complain, as he considered his actions toward her all too lenient.

On the one hand, Ercole seemed to be content with a new confessor Renée had chosen over Pelletier — Fra Miniato, a Dominican friar who had been suspected of heresy in the past. Interestingly, the duke insisted on prolonging his stay in Ferrara when the general of the Dominican Order requested his transfer elsewhere. Maybe the friar represented in his eyes a convenient compromise, pleasing Renée and giving an appearance of religious control at the same time.

On the other hand, Ercole's fears and suspicions were not at all abated. In some of his letters, he confessed that Rome's continual concerns about Renée 'make everyone feel very on edge'. In October 1555, the arrest of Ambrogio Cavalli (c. 1500–1556), a former Augustinian friar who had converted to Protestantism, gave the duke a new chance to scrutinize his wife's court. Cavalli had been in Renée's service for some years, and had just recently returned to

Ferrara (probably sent by Calvin) after spending some time in Geneva. For these reasons, he knew very well the composition of Renée's court and her feelings.

In a message to his ambassador, to be related to the General Inquisitor, Ercole wrote, 'You will also entreat him to examine with torture [that] Lutheran and discover if after Madame our consort had given show of returning to the Catholic faith last year, attending confession and communion, she has had any business or correspondence with those bands, if she has sent any money to those Lutherans as she used to do, and if any more of them have come to see her in Ferrara. [In that case, find out] when, how and who it was, and what kind of person he was.'

From Cavalli's confession, it was obvious that she had maintained her religious convictions and had kept in touch with several reformers in Italy and abroad, continuing to financially support the spreading of the gospel. In other words, Renée was still an important figure in the Italian Reformation, both as a patroness and as a model of Christian ruler. She was not able, however, to save Cavalli from death. When, the following year, in Rome, Cavalli was found guilty of heresy and condemned to the stake, there is no evidence that Renée attempted to intercede.

In July 1558, Calvin was finally able to send a minister to help the duchess, even if for a short time, and continued to exhort her to seek instruction. 'We do not need to urge you,' he said. 'You know well how much you need it.' The letter is full of specific encouragement, reminding Renée that

God sends trials to test our faith, but always gives us the necessary grace and strength to overcome them.

Knowing how oppressively the thought of her failures must have weighed on her shoulders, Calvin reminded her that 'It is good and useful to be aware of our weakness, not to fall into despair, but to be encouraged to find a cure.' Then, as he exhorted her to rule well over her house, following David's example in Psalm 101, he added, 'It is true that, in spite of your efforts, there will always be imperfections. This is why you need to be committed to fulfil this task at least half-way. We have this privilege: when we press toward the goal, God accepts the desire as fact.'

Ercole died suddenly on 3 October 1559. On his deathbed, he urged Renée to promise that she would stop corresponding with Calvin. Apparently, he had included her in his will on condition that she lived 'the Catholic way, as true Christian.' Maybe moved by the pleas of her dying husband, Renée caved in again and promised. Later, Calvin reassured her that, being a mistake with which she had offended God, her promise was not binding, any more than we would consider binding a superstitious vow. He gave as an example the oath made by Herod to grant Herodias' daughter anything she asked. In that case, Herod certainly did not receive any merit for keeping his word. On the contrary, 'This was imputed to him as double condemnation.'

7

BACK TO FRANCE

*In your widowhood, God has made you bolder and freer for
the purpose of drawing you completely to himself*
(John Calvin).

Seeking peace

Soon after Ercole's death, his son Alfonso, then twenty-six, returned to Ferrara from France to become duke
under the name of Alfonso II. In France, he had expressed
his hatred for Protestants, stating that he 'preferred to live
among victims of the plague than among Huguenots [French
Protestants]'. As soon as he returned to Italy, he tightened
his ties with the pope and made plain that heresy would not
be tolerated in his duchy.

Understandably then, he also had some heated arguments
with his mother, mostly over finances, and strong enough
to require the mediation of the French ambassador. All this

undoubtedly encouraged Renée's desire to return to France. Before making a drastic decision, however, she asked Calvin for advice.

The Reformer did not hide his hesitations. France had changed much from 1528. Both Francis I and Henry II had now died, and Henry's son, King Francis II (1544–1560), was a fifteen-year old boy, frail in health and unprepared to rule. Political and religious wars were raging. Calvin warned Renée, 'The government with which they are asking you to meddle is today so confusing that the whole world cries and weeps. If you were part of it and they listened to you, I believe, Madame, that things would not be so bad. But this is not at all what is intended. They want to use your name to foster an evil that is no longer tolerable.'[1]

Most of all, Calvin was not sure how she would fare spiritually. So far, she had seemed ambiguous, vacillating between loyalties. Besides, the strenuous trials she had undergone — with little opportunity to benefit from the comfort and supervision of a local pastor — had left her especially weak. As her spiritual mentor, Calvin pointed out boldly some of the problems that had been hindering her: her love for 'the height and greatness of this world' and her long-standing state of spiritual slumber. Moving to France in that condition was, to him, the equivalent of tempting God, or jumping from the pan into the fire. 'I would be a traitor if I led you to believe that black is white,' he admitted.

If she insisted on leaving, she would soon have to 'embrace a greater commitment' and then 'change, in order to serve

God with discernment, aiming toward the goal, without being entangled in nets that are difficult to break'.

Calvin also checked her motives for moving back to her native soil. If she were looking for rest in her own lands, she had to remember that her 'inheritance and eternal rest are not down here'. Only Jesus Christ, he said, 'is well able to make you forget both France and Ferrara'.

In spite of these warnings, Renée left for France at the end of summer 1560, taking with her almost all the members of her court. On the way, she stopped in Savigliano, in the Piedmont region of Italy, as guest of her niece, Marguerite of Valois (1523–1574), duchess of Savoy. Marguerite and Renée had many things in common. Like Renée, Marguerite was a royal princess (daughter of Francis I and Claude) who had married a duke for political reasons. She had also lost her mother early in life and had been raised by Marguerite of Navarre, who had inspired in her a strong love for humanistic studies, an understanding of the Reformed faith, and an attitude of tolerance in religious matters.

Like Renée, Marguerite of Valois found herself in a very difficult situation. Her sympathies for the Reformed religion had been severely tested on 15 February of the same year when her husband, Emanuele Filiberto I (1528–1580), had issued the Edict of Nice, aimed at repressing the growing community of Protestants in his region (mostly Waldensians). In fact, Renée's visit to Marguerite was due not only to the love she felt for her niece but also to the pleas of a Reformed pastor, Scipione Lentolo (1525–1599), who had been sent by Calvin to Piedmont just before the Edict of Nice. Lentolo asked Renée to intercede with Marguerite.

Renée was not the only one interceding with the young French duchess at that time. While many Protestants had left the region after the edict, some had refused to budge and had been insistently asking for Marguerite's help. Their arguments were convincing: they were not rebelling against the duke, but against the pope, who was imposing a set of doctrines which they considered contrary to God's Word. At first, Emanuele's attempts to buy some time left room for hope. Soon, however, for political rather than religious reasons, he issued orders to attack the Protestants, who had to find refuge in higher Alpine valleys.

In the meantime, Renée resumed her travels, finally arriving, on 7 November 1560, in Orléans, France, where she received a warm official welcome. The king himself had travelled over a mile outside the city to meet her, inviting her to the palace as the royal princess she was.

Trouble in France

It did not take long to realize that Calvin's analysis of the situation in France was correct. The crucial issue was the long and fierce power struggle between two noble families, which had escalated after the death of Henry II. On one hand there was the house of Guise, a ducal family of Roman Catholic persuasion, strongly opposed to the Calvinistic influence in the country, and closely tied to Renée since Francis, Duke of Guise, had married her daughter Anne.

The opposing party was the house of Bourbon, which largely favored the Huguenots.

Renée arrived at the end of the Amboise conspiracy, a failed attempt by the Bourbons to gain power by abducting King Francis II and arresting both the duke of Guise, and his brother Charles, Cardinal of Lorraine (1524–1574). The conspiracy, which ended with the deaths of about 1,500 people, was one of the pivotal events that led up to the French Wars of Religion (1562–1598).

On 5 December 1560, King Francis II died of an ear infection which had spread to his brain. His successor, his ten-year old brother Charles IX (1550–1574), ruled in his place under the direction of their mother, Catherine de' Medici (1519–1589). A Roman Catholic, Catherine was open to reconciliation with the Huguenots, and had adopted a tolerant policy toward them. Her goal was to achieve peace between the factions. The Huguenots, maybe two million at that time, represented about one tenth of the population and were too vocal to be ignored. Far from reaching a fair balance, however, her measures ended up strengthening the political party of the Bourbons over that of the Guise.

Realizing that the political conflicts were too fierce and too entangled with religion to allow her to maintain a position of neutrality, in January 1561, Renée moved to her castle in Montargis, one of the properties she had kept throughout the years. Some see in this choice a desire to emulate Marguerite of Navarre who, by remaining independent and somewhat isolated, had been able to retain the favour of the king while supporting the Protestant cause.

The castle of Montargis, sitting high on a towering hill, was one of the gifts Renée had received from Francis I at her wedding. At her arrival, she described it as 'almost uninhabitable,' requiring an intensive work of remodelling and reconstruction. Within a few years, however, her architect, Jacques Androuet du Cerceau (1510–1584), was able to transform it into a strong and fashionable fortress, with new walls, gracious gardens, ample galleries, a vaulted stairway, and a main hall large enough to require six fireplaces. Altogether, the castle was large enough to host six thousand people.

From its elevated position, the castle overlooked the plains and forests of the Gatinais province on the north and west and the town of Montargis, at the edge of the Loire valley, on the east. Montargis was noted for its unusually wide streets. Like most towns in those days, it was surrounded by a high wall flanked by towers. It was primarily a Catholic town, although its population was more interested in business and trade than in religion.

A proud and independent people, the Montargeois reacted with resistance to Renée's interference in the town's administration. Renée, however, was too conscious of her royal blood to soften her position of sovereignty. Within three years, she was able to gain some control of the local government, personally nominating the magistrates.

While Montargis remained nominally Roman Catholic, within her castle Renée was free to profess her faith, in spite of warnings by her son-in-law, the Duke of Guise, who, according to the Ferrarese ambassador, told her to leave all preaching to the bishops and the clergy. Even her brother-in-law, Cardinal Ippolito II d'Este, who had visited her to convince her to return to the Roman Catholic Church, reportedly wrote, 'As for religion, I have found her most resolute in this new sect, and sorry for her all-too-long pretence.'

Straddling the fence

Calvin, however, was hoping for a greater commitment. When, in December 1560, Jeanne d'Albert (1528–1572), Marguerite's daughter and successor as Queen of Navarre, gave a public profession of the Reformed faith, making Protestantism the official religion in her kingdom, he wrote two letters, one to Jeanne, praising her for her courage, and one to Renée, chiding her for her timidity and urging her to imitate Jeanne's example. Renée, however, was not Jeanne, and repeatedly reminded the Reformer of that reality.

Other Protestants were also perplexed by Renée's reluctance to make a bolder confession and take an open stand for the Huguenots' cause. In June 1561, a Protestant minister suggested again her need for pastoral care. With her agreement and the approval of the Council of Geneva, Calvin sent her a man who had helped her in 1554, during her critical times at the Este court: François de Morel.

From various letters, it seems that the relationship between the princess and Morel was strained from the start. Their personalities were opposite in many ways: he was energetic, daring, and outspoken, while she was cautious, considering peace worth the compromise. Antonio del Corro (1527–1591), who took Morel's place as pastor at Renée's court years later, said that the two 'did not accord any better than fire and water'.

One major issue was the perennial question of the division of church and state. How much authority should rulers concede to church leaders in the administration of their subjects, and how much influence could they claim in the affairs of the church? Renée was determined in two ways. She was not about to turn over her rule over her court, nor to exacerbate her relations with the people of Montargis, who were still mostly Roman Catholic. According to Morel, she told him that no preacher could stay at her house for longer than six months, and that she did not want him to attack the pope, images, or the mass in abusive terms, seeing no advantage in doing so. 'In this case, Monsieur,' he wrote Calvin, 'I have not wished to accept Madame's conditions.'

Renée's rigidity in this occasion may have been caused at least partially by an attempt to abide by a recent royal edict (known as Edict of July) which had been issued on 11 July 1561 as a temporary ceasefire, forbidding the holding of either public or private meetings where sermons were preached or sacraments administered in a way contrary to the teachings of the Roman Catholic Church. As on other occasions, Renée may have thought that a temporary compromise could be beneficial in the long run.

The relations between Renée and Morel improved for a while, especially when she returned from her visit to the conference of Poissy,[2] organized by Catherine de' Medici in order to find a reconciliation between Roman Catholics and Protestants. While Renée did not attend the theological discussions, she was encouraged by the improved position she noticed at court towards Reformed ideas.

Sadly, the conference ended abruptly after only one month, when it became clear that no agreement could be reached. In fact, the conflict between the factions only worsened around the country. The situations varied from town to town. Where Roman Catholics were in the majority, Protestants were persecuted, heavily fined, and often murdered. Where Protestants ruled, churches were sacked, altars destroyed, and Roman Catholics mistreated.

Calvin was strongly opposed to this type of violence. 'God has never commanded to destroy the idols, except in our own homes or, in public, if we have been given the legal authority to do so,' he wrote to the Protestant church in Aix in May 1561. A few years later, he praised Renée for her stand against these abuses. 'I hear you have been solicited to allow the robbing and looting of the papists' shops. I cannot approve of it, regardless of who suggested it, and I praise your virtue and magnanimity in refusing such an unjust request, as well as all the other excesses you mentioned.'

8

CONFLICTS WITHIN AND WITHOUT

I confess, Madame, it is good to fear that God may not let us enjoy his gifts for very long, because each one of us is so interested in himself that we do not know the meaning of bearing with one another with humility and meekness
(John Calvin).

A difficult stand

It was around that time that Calvin wrote Renée a worrisome letter. The supporters of the Roman Catholic Church were gaining strength all over Europe. The pope had entered into a league with the King of Spain and many Italian rulers, including Emanuele Filiberto. 'They believe that they must exterminate from the world all Christianity,' he said.

He was particularly perturbed by the role played by Anne of Este, Renée's daughter, in the French Wars of Religion. 'The Lady of Guise is following a way which, if pursued, will lead only to confusion,' he warned. 'In fact, though she does not see it, she is seeking the ruin of the poor churches in France, which God will protect and maintain. I confess again, Madame, that I would gladly abstain from bothering you, but on the other hand I wish you could influence her, by your authority, to moderate her passions, which she cannot obey without fighting against God.'

We do not have evidence of any correspondence between Renée and her daughter at this time. We know, however, that her feelings as mother were extraordinarily shaken in March 1562, when the duke of Guise and his men attacked a group of Huguenots as they were worshipping in a barn at Vassy, killing thirty and wounding one hundred and fifty. This was not the first act of violence in the French conflict between factions, but it bore a special significance because the duke himself was involved. It has generally been considered the inciting incident officially leading to the French wars of religion. For Renée, it was especially troublesome because the duke was her son-in-law.

'She has received a serious blow from the hateful and cruel outrage committed by her son-in-law,' wrote Morel to Calvin. 'She is full of affection for our brothers and sympathizes with their sufferings, but she cannot keep from wishing her son-in-law well on account of her daughter and she wishes he were less guilty. She is in conflict with herself. A desire exists for the ultimate reign of Christ to triumph over the afflictions of the flesh.'

This 'conflict with herself' never fully abated. While, immediately after these terrible news, she seemed more fervent than ever in favor of the Huguenots' cause, the horrors of war and the pursuit of Christ's kingdom never reconciled in her mind. When escalating violence in Montargis forced her to request the assistance of the Huguenots' armed forces, led by Louis, Prince of Condé (1530–1569), the extent of their brutality and destruction left her appalled. At a time when even Jeanne d'Albret hesitated in her stand, Renée took matters into her hands to defend uncompromisingly her position of neutrality.

Instead of opening her castle to the Huguenot leaders as before, she simply made it available to Protestant refugees who had suffered in the continued war. Withdrawing her support from Condé, she raised a small garrison of soldiers to protect her walls. This caused fiery discussions with Morel, who saw Condé's military actions as justified in order to protect the threatened and abused Protestant community. In his view, Renée could not profess both a love for religious piety and a love for 'impious men who were attacking Christ's church and Gospel, conspiring to kill it and engaging in destroying it' — a clear allusion to the duke of Guise.

The resoluteness of Renée's aversion for the direction the Huguenots had taken is also evident in a long and serious argument she had with Jean de Parthenay (1512–1566), son of Madame de Soubise, during his visit to her castle. Knowing Renée's usual loyalty to friends and family and especially her deep love for her governess, this heated disagreement stands as proof of her determination.

Renée's care for the victims of the conflict soon reached the point that her castle was described as 'a hospital'. Even

Jeanne d'Albret fled to her in the spring of 1562, and later left her son Henri with her for a few months, considering Montargis a safe haven during troubling times. Most Protestant leaders, however, maintained some uncertainties about her commitment.

'[The Queen of] Navarre is very strong,' wrote Theodore Beza to Calvin in January 1563. '[The Duchess of] Ferrara helps the afflicted and serves the church, but she is a woman and her son-in-law is our powerful "friend"'. In other words, it seems that Beza considered her weak and hindered in her true loyalties by her affection for the duke of Guise.

An enemy and a son

This came to a head in February 1563, when her son-in-law, then engaged in a siege of Orléans, decided that the Montargis castle, teeming as it was with Protestants, represented a threat and had to be taken over. The Royal Council agreed. The support and refuge she provided to Protestant refugees was not seen as an act of neutrality but as an encouragement to the Huguenot troops. Finally, they agreed that Renée should be sent to another location for the time being. The duke promptly sent a messenger to give her the unpleasant news, giving as pretext their concern for her protection. Renée stalled for a while, standing her ground on her 'royal' rights. As it turns out, she never had to make a decision. On 24 February 1563, Francis died from a wound inflicted by a Huguenot six days earlier, and the Royal Council never pursued her expulsion.

Renée mourned the duke bitterly. 'He was very dear to me and I loved him as my own son,' she wrote to Catherine de' Medici. In spite of his deeds, various reports of his intervention in protecting some of her Protestant subjects had convinced her that there was a side of him that was not commonly known. 'I know he has persecuted, but I do not believe God reproved him for it, because he gave proof of the contrary before he died,' she wrote Calvin. 'Yet, no one wishes for this knowledge to spread. In fact, they want to put to silence those who know.'

This incident caused Renée to become more vocal than ever, standing up with equal fervour for the defence of her son-in-law and for her Protestant convictions. According to Beza, when she visited the royal court later that year, she employed Reformed ministers to hold public services every day in her apartments and convinced Anne to lead her son Henri in daily prayer and to encourage him to recite portions of Scripture. All this was done in open defiance of Catherine's wishes. In fact, she openly told Catherine that she should attend the services to see things in a different light. Right after Renée's departure, Catherine published an edict forbidding Protestant services in the house of the king.

At home, however, her greatest complaint was against those who kept talking about the duke of Guise as the main cause of the war and as an incorrigible reprobate, undoubtedly doomed to hell. Two things bothered her in particular — the fact that they seemed confidently able to determine what God had decreed regarding his soul, and the fact that they could not stop talking about him, even now that he was dead. In her eyes, this was a sore lack of Christian charity.

Apparently, even while the duke was still alive, some had exhorted her to stop expressing love and saying prayers for him.

As usual, Morel, who had returned to Montargis after a short absence, reported all this to Calvin, and a frequent correspondence ensued between the Reformer and Renée on this subject. While agreeing that no one should ever declare whether a person is in heaven or in hell, 'seeing that there is only one Judge, to whom we all have to give an account', Calvin reminds Renée to maintain a balanced opinion of her son-in-law, considering the facts without letting emotions get the better of her.

Being far from the situation at hand, he exhorted her to judge correctly. When people told her to stop loving the duke and praying for him, what did they really mean? A righteous zeal for the honour of God and the protection of the church, or personal hatred against Francis as an individual? For a Christian, the first is admissible, the second is not. And while Christians should pray for the salvation of their enemies, they cannot pray for their prosperity, nor treat them as brethren.

There is a deep shade of sadness in the Reformer's voice as he reviews the rest of Renée's complaints, too often founded. 'Regarding this, I confess, Madame, it is good to fear that God may not let us enjoy his gifts for very long, because each one of us is so interested in himself that we do not know the meaning of bearing with one another with humility and meekness.'

He encouraged her, however, to persevere in spite of disappointments. 'In any case, Madame, these faults which are giving you pain must not cool your fervour or hinder you in the good path you have undertaken. I know that God has given you enough virtue that you do not need further exhortations. I trust therefore that, in your integrity, you will give an example of charity to those who do not know what charity is, and will confuse those who are false and deceitful toward you.'

Renée was too close to the details to be able to exhibit the poise and composure Calvin advocated. She sent back an impassioned reply. 'I do not believe in my previous letter I have been able to persuade you of my intentions,' she said. Then she proceeded to list all her grievances in great detail, refuting Morel's accusations and complaining that he was too demanding and controlling. Among other objections, she resented how he had organized a consistory of elders in her home to oversee the church, without allowing her to participate in the meetings or to have any say in their decisions. In her opinion, it would have been useful to permit other godly people and ministers to visit from time to time.

Regarding a godly hatred for God's enemies, she agreed with Calvin, but felt it was important to inform him of all the excesses that had been committed against her son-in-law, who had become almost a personification of evil. Just as good men are often idealized and idolized after their death, she felt that the duke had been demonized through a proliferation of exaggerations and inaccuracies which no one seemed to bother checking.

'Monsieur Calvin, it saddens me to see that you do not know how half of the people in this kingdom are behaving and how flattery and envy are ruling here, so much that they exhort simple women to express a desire to kill and strangle with their own hands. This is not the rule given us by Jesus Christ and his apostles. [...] I pray you, Monsieur Calvin, to ask God to show you the truth in all things, as he has showed you before in many respects. I still hope that, through you, God will manifest the hidden malice I see predominant in this world.'

Calvin's last advice

Renée did not know, however, that Calvin's health had deteriorated to a point where he was nearing death. Uncharacteristically for a man who rarely talked about himself, Calvin replied by listing in detail his present ailments. 'Madame, please forgive me if I dictate this letter to my brother, because of my weakness and the pain caused by several illnesses: breathing impediments, [kidney] stones, gout, and an ulcer of the haemorrhoidal veins, preventing every movement with the potential to give me some relief.'

Having received no other recent news on her situation, Calvin was not yet capable of offering a solution to the disagreements. If he was thinking of removing Morel (a decision that seemingly had been on his mind for some time), he could not do it without hearing other opinions. He offered, however, a simple word of advice.

'As to the other topics, Madame, if my advice carries any weight for you, I pray you not to rack your brains over them, as excessive passions always cause much sorrow and close the door to reason and truth.'

Seeing that some of his previous counsel on the duke of Guise had been misinterpreted, he refrained to pursue the subject any further, but left Renée with one encouraging thought. Even if, as she had complained, some had hated her for being the mother-in-law of a well-known enemy of the Protestant church, 'They have all the more loved and honoured you as they have realized that this has not swayed you from an honest and pure profession of Christianity, not only in words, but in the most obvious and tangible way. On my part, I assure you that this has given me the highest admiration of your virtues.'

The letter was dated 4 April 1564. Calvin died twenty-three days later. While we do not have any document describing Renée's feelings at this time, the departure of her faithful mentor must have added a painful blow to her distressed state of mind. Theodore Beza, who took over Calvin's place in Geneva, continued to correspond with the duchess until her death.

9

THE LAST YEARS

*This powerful God, who has no beginning and no end,
through the continuation of his providence, has kept her and
guided her by virtue of the Holy Spirit in this earthly abode,
purely by his goodness and liberality*
(Renée of France).

A small haven in a ravaging war

Morel soon left Montargis, and several preachers took
his place, one after the other. The lack of a constant
pastor at Renée's court must not be attributed necessarily to
friction (since none has been documented), as much as to the
instability of the times. After a brief period of armed peace,
the wars of religion continued to devastate the country.

In Montargis, Renée continued to provide shelter for the
mounting stream of refugees escaping persecution. While
at first she had provided temporary refuge to Protestants en

route to safer countries, by this time her castle had become a permanent haven for families who were not able or willing to start a new life abroad. Families meant children, who needed education as much as food, clothing, and shelter. In line with the high emphasis Calvinism had placed on education, Renée instituted an academy, hiring preceptors and furnishing the classroom with school materials and books.

With time, the academy evolved into a full *collège* — one of the earliest of such institutions in France, since most Protestant leaders were at that time too involved in the wars to devote their time to similar undertakings.

Soon, the increase of the Protestant population at Renée's court became too noticeable for both the population of Montargis and the royal council, who employed several means to put a stop to the situation, even luring Renée to move to the royal court. In September 1568, King Charles IX issued the infamous Edict of St. Maur, prohibiting all religions but Roman Catholicism. The situation for Protestants worsened overnight. They were excluded from public offices and universities, and all pastors were exiled. Besides continuing to offer refuge, Renée intervened to save some imprisoned ministers.

Paul Arrigon, who was Renée's almoner at that time, described the throng of refugees arriving at the castle daily, poor and often ill, requiring care 'as if they were small children. I have visited them in the company of members of the consistory to realize the depth of their misery.' Estimates of the number of refugees housed by Renée at that time vary — some say three hundred, some almost five hundred.

Finally, in February 1569, the Crown took legal action against all Huguenot leaders, including Renée, who was ordered to rid her castle of all Protestants. At this point, the duchess had no alternative but to obey, providing wagons, carriages, and horses needed for the slow exodus of refugees. She remained alone with her Protestant household, waiting for better times.

Clouds gathering for a shattering storm

Better times came in 1570, as the Edict of St. Germain marked a ceasefire in the French wars of religion and allowed Protestants more concessions than ever before. Even if peace did not immediately ensue, the edict provided hope and a respite from full-fledged wars. French Protestant churches flourished, reaching a number of about 1,750 by this time.

In letters to her children, Renée provided a good commentary on the state of France at that time. 'The scars and memories of the troubles will last a long time. May God grant that all things will fall to the glory and honour of the king and to the advantage of the whole kingdom, including those who are afflicted, as I have been in large part, even if I have taken no part in the armed war. I believe that there is no one on either side that has not had his share of damage and destruction, which is becoming clearer as time advances.'

Besides the emotional strain, the wars had caused Renée a dire exhaustion of her funds, to the point that she had to warn her children not to expect anything in inheritance. Her health was also declining.

While she continued to oversee the *collège* and to provide refuge to those in need, Renée spent the last years of her life in closer contact with her family, particularly her daughter Anne, encouraging her to hire Protestant preachers and to continue her biblical studies. In April 1571, she travelled to Paris to visit her son Luigi, who had just arrived from Italy. In spite of Luigi's office as cardinal, Renée had remained very close to him, and he had never openly objected to her religious choices.

While she was in Paris, the first Protestant synod officially sanctioned by the French king took place. Almost all France's leaders participated, including Jeanne d'Albret. Renée's absence signalled once again her indifference to political parties and decisions.

Renée returned to Paris a few times to visit Anne. She was there in August 1572, when tension was mounting over the growing power of Gaspard de Coligny (1519–1572), the principal Protestant leader, and over the unexpected and controversial wedding of Protestant Henry of Navarre (1553–1610), who was to become king Henry IV, to Catholic Marguerite of Valois (1553–1615), daughter of Catherine de' Medici and Henry II. The wedding, supposedly designed to bring together the two rival factions, was celebrated on 18 August without significant disturbances.

Four days later, however, Coligny, who had remained in Paris after the wedding to discuss some developments from the Edict of St Germain, was nearly killed by a bullet shot from an upstairs window in the Louvre. The would-be assassin escaped, and to this day no one has been able to assess who was ultimately behind the attempted murder. (As typical in this type of crime mysteries, many suggestions have been made, including Anne, as part of the house of Guise, and Catherine de' Medici.)

The incident sparked the infamous St Bartholomew's Day Massacre, a group of assassinations (including that of Coligny) followed by a massive chain of acts of violence against all Protestants — men, women, and children. The extent of the carnage was such that the River Seine — it was reported — ran red with Protestant blood. Very few of the Protestant nobles who had remained in Paris after the wedding survived. Apparently, Renée remained hidden for about a week, then left quickly and under escort, taking some Huguenots with her. She arrived in Montargis on 31 August.

In July 1573, the Edict of Boulogne restricted the privileges previously awarded to Protestants. In September, the king went as far as ordering everyone to attend the Catholic Mass. Anne, who had kept her mother informed, warned her at this time, 'There is no one, no matter how great, who has not attended [Mass]. Madame, [if you do not comply], do not doubt that they will take your servants.'

We do not know the extent of Renée's compliance. In conformity with her character, she probably attended Mass to avoid problems. Still, her name does not appear in the list of apostates published by the church in Geneva, and, in October, Catherine de' Medici was still trying to persuade her to return to the Roman Catholic faith.

A quiet departure

The greatest proof of Renée's religious convictions rests however in her last will, a document first written in 1573 and revised several times, where she professed her faith and ordered the manner of her burial, which was to be carried out with no ceremony or pomp in the small chapel by her castle. Her instructions were specific and detailed.

Finally, on 12 June 1575, after succumbing to a respiratory illness, this princess who had always been ready to remind everyone of her royal status, was buried — according to her wishes — in a simple wooden coffin, carried by six common men and interred without constructions or tombstones.

When Anne, warned of the news, arrived at Montargis, she was upset to see that the burial had taken place without her presence or intervention. In one last act of homage, she gave orders that candles must burn in Renée's chapel night and day. Both she and Luigi also pressed the royal court to give Renée a proper funeral, as suitable for a princess, but the king denied it, because Renée had not died in the true religion.

In Italy, Renée's death caused Alfonso further embarrassment, as she not only died a heretic, but left him no inheritance at all (the castle and all her possessions had been bequeathed entirely to Anne). Obviously upset, he questioned whether it was permissible for a heretic to make a legal will, but was informed that in France, unlike in Italy, that was in fact the case. He also worried, as always, about appearances in the eyes of the Catholic Church and the Italian people. 'In Italy, and especially in Rome,' he wrote, 'there is much strange talk. In fact, if she had at least been buried according to the Catholic rites, we could have disguised it and the offices could have been said.'

Renée died as she lived, quietly and according to her conscience. Due to frequent revisions, we have five versions of her last will, in three languages (French, Italian, and Latin). Each version is slightly different, but the main message is the same. Written in the third person, her will contains a confession of Renée's sins and an acknowledgment of God's grace and mercy in rescuing her and allowing her to know the truth. In spite of her vacillation and serious falls, she gave God the glory for the preservation of her faith, recognizing that 'this powerful God, who has no beginning and no end, through the continuation of his providence, has kept her and guided her by virtue of the Holy Spirit in this earthly abode, purely by his goodness and liberality, for which she is more obliged and indebted than she may be able to say or appreciate, and for which she must give him continually her most humble thanks.'

10

CALVIN AND RENÉE

I know well how much respect [John Calvin] has had for you during all of his life, having taught and confirmed to you the doctrine of truth longer than any Lady still living today (Theodore Beza, French Reformer).

The correspondence between John Calvin and Renée is interesting for several reasons. First of all, it lasted from 1537, the year after they met, until his death in 1564 — the longest and most pastoral correspondence the Reformer ever kept with a noblewoman. Second, it shows a different side of Calvin, as not just a devoted pastor but a personal pastor, who sympathizes and shares details of his own struggles.

The detailed list of his ailments in his last letter to Renée, for example, reveals the unique level of familiarity he had with the duchess. While normally reticent to describe his physical ailments (whether because of a natural aversion to talking about himself or, as some have suggested, because his enemies had interpreted some of them, such as gout, as a sign of luxurious living), this time Calvin gives the duchess the complete inventory, as a man would with a dear friend.

Calvin's correspondence with Renée is also interesting because it shows what issues were particularly significant to a young Reformed church: the acceptance or refusal of the Catholic Mass, the common fear of making an open profession of Protestant doctrines ('nicodemism' — see second section below), the importance of church government and discipline, and the ever questioned relationship between church and state.

Interestingly, many of these issues have resurfaced today, and the exchange between these two sixteenth-century believers may be more relevant than we may at first expect.

The Mass — sacrilege and idolatry?

Renée's demands that her court attend the Roman Catholic Mass were the catalyst for Calvin's first letter to her. From his description of the events, gathered from at least one report, it seems that Renée's chaplain Richardot had taught her that the issue was a matter of Christian liberty.

The Mass, a bastion of Catholic medieval doctrine and practice, had been denounced by Reformers for decades as a sacrilegious pretence to repeat Christ's sacrifice. In 1534, the posting of handbills attacking this ceremony had provoked a large-scale repression of Protestants in France. Calvin himself had expounded this subject exhaustively in his *Institutes of the Christian Religion*, and probably discussed it at length during his visit to Renée in 1536; so much so that in this letter he feels confident of her understanding of this matter. Still, he devotes two paragraphs of his first letter to its exposition, explaining in a clear and concise manner why he considers the Mass as both a sacrilege ('the most abominable sacrilege one can imagine') and an act of idolatry.

To describe how the Mass is a sacrilege and a blasphemy, Calvin quotes the Roman Catholic Canon which defines it a sacrifice for the redemption of both living and dead.[1] To Calvin, this is a subversion of Christ's sacrifice on Calvary, where he paid for the sins of his people once and for all. If the Mass is a sacrifice that has to be repeated by the church, how can we say that Christ's sacrifice was effective? Calvin led Renée to consider the Scriptures, particularly Hebrews 9:26: 'He has appeared once for all at the end of the ages to put away sin by the sacrifice of himself.'

Second, Calvin called the Mass an act of idolatry, because, as he had previously explained in his *Institutes*, it promotes worship of the created means rather than of God, and trust in the physical objects for the forgiving of sins rather than in Christ's sacrifice on the cross. In fact, for Calvin, the Mass is the worst kind of idolatry because it is not just a simple worshipping of idols, as pagans may do, but a worshiping of idols in the name of Christ. He reminds Renée of God's great wrath on 'those who bow down and swear to the Lord and yet swear by Milcom' (Zephaniah 1:5).

Nicodemism — a private faith

Another important issue addressed by Calvin in his first letter to Renée is the attitude of those who outwardly conformed to the Roman Catholic tenets while concealing their Protestant beliefs. Later,[2] Calvin called those people 'Nicodemites', because they took as justification the biblical example of Nicodemus, a Jewish rabbi who came to Jesus by night for fear of the Jews (John 3:2). In spite of coining the name, Calvin explained that Nicodemus was not a coward, because he sided openly with Jesus after his death, burying him when even the disciples had deserted him.

In many countries at that time, Protestants were left with three options: declare their faith and face death, go into voluntary exile in a country allowing Protestant worship, or keep their heads down. Since the first two options were definitely not easy, many believers throughout Europe were debating whether the third option might be a possibility where circumstances seemed to warrant it.

They gave several justifications. Some misconstrued Scriptures, such as Romans 14:22 ('The faith that you have, keep between yourself and God') to justify their behaviour. In Richardot's case, he taught that 'Exterior things are not important, as long as the heart is right.' Calvin's answer is ready and to the point: 'To this, our Lord replies that he wants to be glorified in our body, which he has redeemed through his blood, and this requires our confession with our mouths and our absolute devotion to his honour, being unpolluted and undefiled by that which is displeasing to him.'

In other words, as he explained in other writings, Christ has redeemed both our souls and our bodies and is now Lord over both. The way in which we physically serve and worship God cannot then be considered insignificant, and the confession of the heart cannot be separated from the confession with the mouth.

Apparently, Richardot had convinced Renée that attending Mass was not only permissible but even advisable whenever the refusal to attend could potentially offend weaker Christians. This was for Calvin a perversion of biblical passages such as Romans 14:20-23 and 1 Corinthians 8:13 and 10:25-33. He explained that these biblical commands 'concern issues of small importance, which are irrelevant and allowed in our liberty'. On the other hand, 'Concerning things that are commanded or forbidden by God, even if the whole world became offended, we must not transgress his orders'.

Besides, even our liberty in unimportant matters is always intended to edify our neighbour, not to cause him to fall, and by attending the Mass, Renée was endangering those around her. 'If we know that the Mass is accursed and execrable, and we attend it to please the ignorant, those who see us there will conclude that we approve it and will follow our example.' What is more, 'If we wish to avoid every occasion of offending other people, we would have to cast out Jesus Christ, who is the rock of offence on which most people trip and fall.'

Church government and discipline

John Calvin had a very high view of the visible church. On the heels of the early Fathers, particularly Augustine, he saw the church as a mother for the believers, one which cannot be abandoned or neglected. He had earlier written, 'For such is the value which the Lord sets on the communion of his church, that all those who contumaciously alienate themselves from any Christian society, in which the true ministry of his word and sacraments is maintained, he regards as deserters of religion. So highly does he recommend her authority, that when it is violated he considers that his own authority is impaired.'[3]

For a princess like Renée, highly conscious of her status and authority, who had been used to claiming her rights against unjust demands by her husband, submitting even partially the government of her home to a few members of the local church was a rather arduous task, especially since they were fallible men whose ideas often contrasted with hers. Still, Calvin kept bringing her back to the authority of the church, reminding her that problems and scandals in her court required both her vigilance and her support of church discipline. He wrote:

> I pray you, keep as much as possible a firm hand in order to maintain a good vigilance and suppression of vices and scandals. By this, I do not mean so much human vigilance, as rather the supervision of the church consistory and the certainty that those who are established as moral overseers are God-fearing individuals, living a holy life, being so honest and bold that nothing may prevent them from doing their

duty, and having the necessary zeal to fully preserve God's honour. May no one, whatever their position or state, however you may esteem them and whatever opinion you may have of them, be ashamed of submitting to the order established by the Son of God himself and of bending their necks to accept his yoke.

Church discipline was for Calvin an integral part of the Reformation:

To have a duly reformed church, it is more than necessary that someone be in charge of watching over each life. So that no one may feel burdened by this accountability to the elders who are responsible, let them be chosen by the church. This prerogative must in fact be preserved, and those who are suitable and qualified must be chosen with great prudence and approved by the consistory.

As far as Renée's authority was concerned, Calvin believed she had to exercise authority as a ruler over her house but not over the church. In particular, she was not to hinder proper church discipline when necessary.

I am not saying that, if there is a scandal among your people, you, being the most prominent member of the church, should not be warned first, so that you may wisely correct it. Rather, your authority should not hinder the course of discipline. If your servants are spared, the consistory's authority would dissolve as water.

Calvin did not request that Renée absent herself from the consistory meetings, as Morel had wished, but only that she submit to their authority, without interfering with their decisions. He also did not seem to concern himself with the fact that she was a woman. 'How will the Papists and Anabaptists scoff to see us run by women?' Morel had cried in a letter to Calvin regarding this situation, just a month earlier. In spite of his view of women rulers as an occasional necessary evil, however, Calvin maintained his conviction that, once in power, they had to be respected for their office.

Loving our enemies and the unity of the Testaments

After the death of the Duke of Guise, someone apparently exhorted Renée to overcome her natural motherly love for him, realizing that, as an enemy of God's people, he had to be hated as David hated his enemies. Interpreting one of Calvin's letters as an endorsement of this thought, Renée complained that hating our enemies was allowed in David's day but is no longer acceptable. To this, Calvin quickly raises a warning flag, eager to avert any suggested dichotomy between the Old Testament and the New. 'Madame, this argument would lead to the overthrowing of the whole Scripture, and for that reason we should shun it as we would a deadly plague.'

Pitting the New Testament against the Old is, for Calvin, a deadly practice. In his view, if there is a dichotomy, it is not between the Old and New Testament, nor between David's desire to see God's enemies destroyed and Jesus' command to love our enemies, but rather between 'an upright, pure, and well-regulated zeal' against those who oppose God's kingdom and a personal hatred for individuals.

'We all agree,' he explained, 'that as children of God we must conform ourselves to his example, striving to do good to those who are unworthy of it, just as he causes his sun to shine on the evil and the good. Thus hatred and Christianity are things incompatible.'

Here, however, he makes an important distinction. 'I mean hatred towards persons, in opposition to the love we owe them. On the contrary, we are to wish and even procure their good, and to labour, as much as in us lies, to maintain peace and concord among us.'

Calvin tried to live according to this rule. 'For my own part,' he said, 'though I have often prayed that God should have mercy on [the duke of Guise], yet it is certain I have often desired that God should lay his hand on him in order to deliver out of his hands the poor church, unless it pleased God to convert him.' He explained to Renée that his exhortations had actually stopped some eager men of war from killing the duke much sooner.

At the same time, Calvin clarified that our love for an individual who is fighting against the church should not supersede our duty to protect our brethren. 'St. John, of whom you have only retained the charitable words, clearly shows that we ought not, under show of affection for men, become indifferent to the duty we owe to the honour of God and the preservation of his church.'

How can we walk this fine line between a righteous zeal against God's enemies and our love for them as individuals? For Calvin, 'three things are requisite: first, that we should have no regard for ourselves nor our private interests; next, that we should possess prudence and discretion not to judge at random; and finally, that we observe moderation not to exceed the bounds of our calling.'

He reminded Renée that he had repeated this concept several times in his Commentary to the Psalms, showing that if David sought to retaliate against injustice, it was never as an individual, but always and only as a king. For example, in his commentary to Psalm 41:10, Calvin wrote:

> *If, then, each individual indiscriminately, in taking vengeance upon his enemies, should allege the example of David in his own defence, it is necessary, first, to take into account the difference which subsists between us and David, by reason of the circumstances and position in which he was placed by God; and, secondly, it is necessary to ascertain whether the same zeal which was in him reigns also in us, or rather, whether we are directed and governed by the same divine Spirit. David, being king, was entitled, in virtue of his royal authority, to execute the vengeance of God against the wicked; but as to us, our hands are tied.*

Our weakness, God's sanctification

Calvin's realism about human nature is deeply comforting. We can especially appreciate it today, as a constant barrage of self-improvement messages (even from Christian sources) drives us to reach for our inner potential, leaving many discouraged and exhausted.

Calvin reminds Renée that we are by nature weak and sinful. Her denial of her faith had been sorely disappointing, but not beyond remedy. When God allows his children to fall, Calvin explains, it is never with the intention of destroying them or casting them into despair. On the contrary, as we have noted earlier, he gives them double strength to resume the fight.

Even this resuming of the fight, however, is seen by Calvin with lucid realism and attainable expectations. His view of sanctification is well-balanced. Christians are, as Luther explained, both justified and sinful, and live in the 'already but not yet', enjoying God's grace and strength in a yet incomplete fashion. For this reason, Calvin reminds Renée not to expect perfection or quick results. Knowing that the process is always slow and Christians never achieve one hundred per cent obedience in this life, he is content if she can 'commit to discharge [her] duty at least halfway', reminding her that God accepts the desire to do his will as the actual accomplishment.

He also guards the duchess against discouragement over the conflicts and inconsistencies that are in every human heart. 'If you find in yourself some contradiction,' he writes, 'do not be surprised.' He reminds her that Jesus, referring to Peter's violent death, once told him, 'Another [...] will carry you where you do not want to go' (John 21:18).

Calvin explains this verse further in his commentary on the Gospel of John.

It may be thought strange that Christ should say that Peter's death will not be voluntary; for, when one is hurried unwillingly to death, there is no firmness and none of the praise of martyrdom. But this must be understood as referring to the contest between the flesh and the Spirit, which believers feel within themselves; for we never obey God in a manner so free and unrestrained as not to be drawn, as it were, by ropes, in an opposite direction, by the world and the flesh. Hence that complaint of Paul, 'The good that I would, I do not, but the evil that I would not, that I do' (Romans 7:19).

'We see, then,' he continues in his letter, 'that we will never serve God without arguing, because our flesh recoils from the fight.'

If then we are so weak and incapable of even desiring to serve God, why and how does Calvin think Renée should try to do it? Out of gratitude for what God has done through Christ and by relying on his Spirit, in view of his promises. He explains:

I know that the same assaults that caused you to fall will repeat themselves, and that very soon, but I beg you to think how much you owe to him who has redeemed you at such a high price and how every day he invites you to his heavenly inheritance. God is not a master to serve with reservations, especially if we consider the end result of all our sufferings, among disgrace and affliction, for his name. Appeal to him then, trusting that only he is sufficient to relieve our frailty, and meditate on these beautiful promises he has made to raise us to the hope of the heavenly glory. In fact, just a taste of that glory is enough to make us forget the world and place it under our feet.

If it is true that now we live in the 'not yet' as sinners, Calvin strongly reminds Renée that we live also in the 'already' as justified believers, and constantly points her away from herself and her failures, and to Christ.

> Pressing toward the goal is not in vain, although you may still be far from it, because our race is sure as long as we follow God, even in weakness. And this certainty must strengthen us to overcome every temptation.

The discharge of duties

In spite of our frailties, we still need to discharge our duties, as Calvin reminds Renée frequently in his letters. In her case, this meant oversight over her household (and, in Montargis, over her subjects), a task which Calvin deemed extremely important, not only in obedience to God's Word (he reminds her of Psalm 101), but also as a means to put to silence any slander. This exhortation to be blameless in the sight of others was particularly significant during the Reformation, when Roman Catholics sought every opportunity to prove that a doctrine of salvation only by grace and only through faith inevitably produced debauchery and dissolution.

This was really the same argument that Paul mentioned rhetorically in Romans 6:15, when he asked, 'What then? Are we to sin because we are not under law but under grace? By no means!' The fact that God saved us purely by his grace without any of our merits really moves us to obey, not deter us. In fact, it motivates us to obey for the right reasons (out of gratitude) and not out of fear of punishment or desire for rewards. This is something the Reformers had truly experienced in their own lives and were eager to prove.

Calvin's exhortations to the duchess to keep her house in order were motivated by frequent concerns raised by Morel and others. In a series of seven letters Morel wrote to Calvin in the summer of 1561, for example, he lamented Renée's reluctance to reprove one of her servants and her resistance to allowing the consistory to exercise church discipline. He repeated his complaints two years later, adding that the duchess preferred to send her transgressing servants away rather than to permit an investigation of their actions. In a letter to Renée, Calvin gives an example of one of these problems — the case of a young man who had left his wife to go after a loose woman.

In exhorting the duchess to keep a stricter watch on her subjects and to allow the consistory to perform its God-given duties, Calvin is, however, able to sympathize with her struggles. Keeping order in one's house is never unproblematic. It is always easier to ignore sin than to face it and correct it. Calvin knew that Renée would have many obstacles to face — not only her natural resistance to authority and her apparent incompatibility with Morel, but also much opposition from her subjects. In fact, one feels that he spoke from experience when he mentioned how 'people are obstinate' and ready to slander without cause. After all, it was he who, faced with the prospect of returning to pastor the abusive population of Geneva, said, 'Rather would I submit to death a hundred times than to that cross, on which one had to perish daily a thousand times over.'

We know, however, that Calvin returned to Geneva when called, submitting to the cross he so terribly dreaded. It was with deep conviction of the sufficiency of God's strength that he could exhort Renée to do the same. 'I beseech you, Madame, to get used to being criticized for doing good, for this is the salary that is promised to us from on high,' he warned her. On the other hand, he also exhorted her to 'Rejoice, as you have reason to do so among so much sadness, because to be so approved by God as to be chosen as an instrument of his glory is not a small gain.'

Notes

Chapter 1

1. These lines of poetry play on the name Renée, which means 'born again'. Here is the original version: 'Née deux fois de nom et d'ame/Enfant de roy par sa naissance/ Enfant du ciel par cognaissance de celui qui la sauvera.'
2. Sack of Rome, 6 May 1527.
3. Andrea Doria (1466–1560).
4. See Martin Luther, *The Estate of Marriage* (1522). John Calvin was stricter in this respect, allowing the wife to leave the husband only if she was at risk of losing her life.
5. In the original: 'Ha, Marguerite, écoute la suffrance/Du noble coeur de Renée de France/Puis comme soeur plus fort que d'espérance/Console-la!'

Chapter 2

1. Chaplain in charge of distributing alms.
2. A further explanation of Calvin's arguments on the Mass and Christian liberty is found in chapter ten of this book.

Chapter 3

1. Salvatore Caponetto, *The Protestant Reformation in Sixteenth-Century Italy*, trans. Anne C. Tedeschi and John Tedeschi, Thomas Jefferson University Press, 1999, p.25.

Chapter 4

1. The word 'Lutheran' was often used at that time to describe Protestants in general.
2. Sic.
3. Antonio Musa Bresavola, one of the most illustrious Italian physicians of that time.

Chapter 7

1. *Calvini Opera*, XVIII, ep. 3228, coll. 147-148.
2. Colloquy of Poissy, from 9 September to 9 October 1561.

Chapter 10

1. *Cf.* Canon 901. We can understand what Calvin meant if we read, for example, the *Catechism of the Council of Trent, published by command of Pope Pius the Fifth,* trans. Rev. J. Donovan, Fielding Lucas Jr, Baltimore, 1829, p.175: 'The Holy sacrifice of the Mass, therefore, is not only a sacrifice of praise and thanksgiving, or a commemoration of the sacrifice on the cross, but also *a sacrifice of propitiation by which God is appeased and rendered propitious* [italics added for emphasis].' Today, although the Roman Catholic Church specifies that the Mass and the sacrifice of Christ on the cross are 'one single sacrifice', they still maintain that this sacrifice is in both cases propitiatory.
2. John Calvin, *Excuse à Messieurs les Nicodémites* (1544).
3. John Calvin, *Institutes of the Christian Faith*, IV.1.

BIBLIOGRAPHY

Renée's life, as well as the Reformation in Italy and France in general, only caught the full attention of historians in the 19th century, when Thomas MacCrie, in his *History of the Progress and the Suppression of the Reformation in Italy in the Sixteenth Century* (Philadelphia: Presbyterian Board of Publication, 1829), names Renée among the supporters of the Reformation. Until last century, Emmanuel Rodocanachi, *Renée de France, une protectrice de la Réforme en Italie et en France* (Paris: Ollendorff,1896; reprinted Genève: Slatkine, 1970), and Bartolommeo Fontana's *Renata di Francia Duchessa di Ferrara, sui documenti dell'Archivio Estense, del Mediceo, del Gonzaga e dell'Archivio Segreto Vaticano* (Rome: Forzani, 1893; reprinted Nabu Press, 2012) have been the most comprehensive works on the duchess. Fontana, however, strongly defends his opinion of her as a weak Roman Catholic deceived by profiteering Protestants. He is still worth reading for the abundance of primary sources and as a key to understanding how Renée's fluctuations have led some to claim her as a victimized daughter of the Church of Rome.

While the nineteenth century also produced a large number of fictionalized or semi-fictionalized works on Renée (generally portraying her as a Protestant heroine), twentieth-century historians have delivered more well-balanced views. The most accurate works of the century are arguably the writings of Charmarie Jenkins Blaisdell (Webb): 'Renée of France Between Reform and Counter-Reform', *Gütersloher* (1972); 'Politics and Heresy in Ferrara', *The Sixteenth Century Journal*, vol. 6, nr. 1 (April 1975), pp. 67-93; and *Royalty and Reform: the Predicament of Renée of France 1510-1575*, unpublished doctoral dissertation, Tuft University (October 1969).

Blaisdell's works are not readily accessible (they are mostly available only through library inter-loan programmes), but are worth the effort for a serious study of Renée's life. Blaisdell has devoted much time to research in this field in Italy, France, and Switzerland, enriching the existing wealth of primary sources with new and invaluable discoveries. Through her studies, Blaisdell calls Fontana's depiction of a duchess victoriously brought back to the Roman Catholic fold unfounded and mostly based on the boasts made by Pelletier to Loyola.

While she denies that Renée ever had the leadership skills, radical religious devotion, and even intellectual prowess of other noblewomen of her time, she acknowledges her importance in the religious scene of sixteenth-century Europe and the sincerity of her adherence to basic Protestant doctrines. Blaisdell's works are also particularly valuable in understanding the strong influence of political events on Renée's life and choices.

A brief summary of Renée's life is given by Roland H. Bainton, *Women of the Reformation in Italy and Germany* (Boston: Beacon Press, 1971), pp. 235-251. Its companion book, Roland Bainton, *Women of the Reformation in France and England* (Minneapolis: Augsburg Fortress Press, 1973; reprinted Lima, OH: Academic Renewal Press, 2001) may be useful as a brief overview of the role of women in the French Reformation. To understand Renée in the context of the Italian Reformation, a valuable volume is Salvatore Caponetto, *The Protestant Reformation in Sixteenth-Century Italy*, translated by Anne C. Tedeschi and John Tedeschi (Kirksville, MO: Thomas Jefferson University Press, 1999).

For those interested in reading the full version of Calvin's letters to Renée, they are available in English through Jules Bonnet's translation (there are various editions of this work) or in the original French in *Joannis Calvini opera quae superiant omnia* (also online through the Hekman Library). F. Whitfield Barton, *Calvin and the Duchess* (Louisville: Westminster/John Knox Press, 1989), includes Bonnet's translation of most of the correspondence between Renée and Calvin (eleven letters by the Reformer and one by the duchess). Contrary to most historians' conclusions, Barton believes Renée never capitulated to Pelletier, but produced a document signed by Pope Paul III which allowed her to be tried exclusively by the Roman religious court, and Ercole preferred to lie about her conversion rather than to turn her over to the Inquisition. While Barton's book is easy to read, it is not included in most lists of reliable historical sources because of her choice to emend and paraphrase some important original documents.

As an Italian speaker, I was able to profit from Leonardo De Chirico, Daniel Walker, *Lealtà in tensione. Un carteggio protestante tra Ferrara e l'Europa* (Caltanisetta: Alfa e Omega, 2009), containing an Italian translation of all the available correspondence between Renée and Calvin (twelve letters from the Reformer and three from the duchess), and a well-documented account of her life, based on both primary and secondary sources.

Also very useful (still in Italian) were several studies included in *Rivista Schifanoia*, a journal published by the Istituto di Studi Rinascimentali di Ferrara; particularly Rosanna Gorris Camos, 'Donne ornate di scienza e di virtù, donne francesi alla corte di Renata di Francia', *Rivista Schifanoia*, Istituto di Studi Rinascimentali di Ferrara, nr. 28/29, pp. 175-205; Chiara Franceschini, 'Literarum studia nobis communia, Olimpia Morata e la corte di Renata di Francia', *Rivista Schifanoia*, Istituto di Studi Rinascimentali di Ferrara, nr. 28/29, pp. 207-232; and Eleonora Belligni, 'Reti eterodosse e maestri d'eresia: la corte di Renata di Francia tra Ferrara e Consandolo', *Rivista Schifanoia*, Istituto di Studi Rinascimentali di Ferrara, nr. 28/29, pp. 233-246.

Corollary studies can be found in Charmarie Jenkins Blaisdell, 'Calvin's Letters to Women: The Courting of Ladies in High Places', in *The Sixteenth Century Journal*, Vol. 13, 1982, 3, pp. 67-84; and Nancy Lyman Roetker, 'The Role of Noblewomen in the French Reformation', ARG 63 (1972). My main disagreement with Blaisdell is that she believes that Calvin's interest in Renée was mostly motivated by political concerns and that her ambivalence infuriated him, while his writings seem to me to convey a more pastoral and caring approach.